The Ope

y

Book 1

Analysing Business Cases

Prepared for the course team by Jim Donohue,
Lina Adinolfi and Prithvi Shrestha

This publication forms part of an Open University course LB160 *Professional communication skills for business studies*. Details of this and other Open University courses can be obtained from the Student Registration and Enquiry Service, The Open University, PO Box 197, Milton Keynes MK7 6BJ, United Kingdom: tel. +44 (0)845 300 60 90, email general-enquiries@open.ac.uk

Alternatively, you may visit the Open University website at www.open.ac.uk where you can learn more about the wide range of courses and packs offered at all levels by The Open University.

To purchase a selection of Open University course materials visit http://www.ouw.co.uk, or contact Open University Worldwide, Michael Young Building, Walton Hall, Milton Keynes MK7 6AA, United Kingdom for a brochure. tel. +44 (0)1908 858793; fax +44 (0)1908 858787; email ouw-customer-services@open.ac.uk

The Open University
Walton Hall, Milton Keynes
MK7 6AA

First published 2008. Second edition 2009

Edited and designed by The Open University.

Typeset by Pam Callow, S&P Enterprises Ltd.

Printed in the United Kingdom by Cambrian Printers, Aberystwyth

ISBN 978 0 7492 2541 4

2.1

Contents

The course team

Lina Adinolfi (author)

Haider Ali (OU Business School advisor)

Liz Benali (course manager)

Jim Donohue (course team chair)

Elizabeth J. Erling (course team member)

Helen Peters (author)

Prithvi Shrestha (author)

Production team

Mandy Anton (graphic designer)

Ann Carter (print buyer)

Peter Lee (editor)

Jon Owen (graphic artist)

Simon Rodwell (media project manager)

Amanda Smith (editor)

Nikki Tolcher (media assistant)

Consultant authors

Derek Davies (University of Manchester)

David Lewis (DML Communication Services, The Netherlands)

External assessor

George Blue (University of Southampton)

Critical readers

Olwyn Alexander (Heriot-Watt University)

David Hann (E301 and E303 tutor)

Dennis Beer (B200 tutor)

Malcolm Harris (B200 tutor)

Mary Lewis (B200 tutor)

Peter Martin (B200 tutor)

Brian Terry (B200 tutor)

Geraldine Wooley (B200 tutor)

Acknowledgements

We would like to thank the following former B200 students for their contribution to the course design:

Dimitri Billaud

Vera Brenner

Carmen Jaffke

Klaus Konwalin

Gareth Price

Jitendra Ranpura

Caroline Siddall

Tibebu Tefeta

Thanks also go to the following business school students for giving us permission to use their assignments as examples of good practice:

Wayne Barker

Rebecca Britain

Anne Buckingham

Rebecca Chadwick

Assumpta Corley

Lee Farndon

Nicola Fink

Stephanie Firth

Jenny Frister

Ruth Fulton

Rupert Groves

Claire Houlden

Emma Kingston

Tom Laverick

John Lyons

Daniel McCarthy

Nicola McKee

Damian Millington

Ian Pegg

Noel Rafferty

David Sharp

Yoshie Shinoyama

Jenny Sprackling

Martin Surrey

Angela Temple

Christine Thomas

Amanda Todd

Debbie Walker

SESSION 1 Mapping the case

1.1 Introduction

When you start a business studies course, it is usually not long before you have to read a case study. Case studies come in different shapes and sizes but they all have the same purpose. They present a part of the business world for you to think about using ideas from the business studies course.

Sometimes you don't have to do more than read them. Sometimes you have to study them more carefully and write an assignment on them. This process forms the title of this book: *Analysing Business Cases*.

Analysis is a key word. One book says if you are not really sure about what a case study is, don't worry; when your tutor gives you something and says, 'Analyse that for next Tuesday', that's a case study (Easton, 1992, p. 1).

The purpose of this book is to help you develop the skills to do analysis.

Learning outcomes

In this session, you will:

- meet the six skills needed to analyse a business case
- read a business case and make notes on it
- develop your reading and note-making skills
- be introduced to the ways in which case study texts are organised
- develop language for analysing business performance in the airline industry
- apply the skills you have learned to other business cases
- discuss your experience with other students on the course.

1.2 What is a case study?

The first thing to say about case studies is that they are texts. **Text** is an important word in the study of professional communication so you need to be clear from the start what is meant by it.

A text is a collection of words

This course focuses on skills with words, particularly written words. However, usually a word on its own does not mean very much. It only has meaning in a text. If you look around where you are now, you can probably see some texts. I can see the following texts: a lot of books, an old Christmas card with the words 'We Three Kings' on the front of it, a medicine bottle with the words 'Atomize Spray, Keep out of the reach of children', a letter from a book company, and a piece of paper with a telephone number and company name which I wrote yesterday.

The words in a text have meaning because the text is in a situation

Each of these texts is complete and communicates meaning **in its situation**. If the words 'Keep out of the reach of children' were written on the front of the Christmas card, it would be difficult to understand their meaning. On the side of a medicine bottle, the meaning is obvious. Each of the texts mentioned above has a situation in which it belongs. If you don't know the situation, it can be very difficult to understand the text. 'We Three Kings' may have a meaning if you are familiar with the story of Christmas but, if not, that three-word text is meaningless.

Particular texts can be grouped into types of texts

The texts mentioned above have been grouped into types: letter, Christmas card, medicine bottle instruction, book. As soon as I say what type of text it is, you can probably fit it with your own idea of these text types. Even the piece of paper with the telephone number and the name of a company is a type of text. It could be called 'a note written before telephoning a company' text.

Texts are organised

If you try to visualise the texts mentioned above, part of what you see is probably differences in the ways the words are laid out. A letter is organised differently from a book or a medicine bottle instruction. They are organised differently because they are different text types for different situations.

So when a case study is said to be a text, it means that this collection of words has been organised into a particular text-type in order to communicate in a particular situation. In the next section you will look more closely at what type of text a case study is.

1.3 What type of text is a case study text?

In Activity 1.1 below, you will look at one or two paragraphs from four different case study texts.

The activity asks you to think about six features of these case studies. The first three are about the text itself:

Content: is it about a person, an organisation or a whole industry?

Organisation: is it like a story with a sequence of events happening one after the other, or is it a description with no time sequence?

Language: is it formal or informal, personal or impersonal?

The second three features are about the situation:

Writer: is it a business studies lecturer or a journalist?

Reader: is the writer writing for students or for the general public?

Purpose: is it for education, entertainment or information?

Activity 1.1

Purpose: to look at some features of case studies.

Task: in Resource Book 1 there are four extracts from case study texts (Extracts 1.1 to 1.4). Underneath each extract there is a table of features. For each extract, tick the features you think best describe the extract. You don't have to understand these texts in detail.

Compare your answers with those suggested in the Answer section at the end of this session.

Comment

The four extracts show features of case study texts. For example, case studies describe or tell a story about a part of the business world. They can be written by lecturers or by newspaper journalists. Noticing features such as these can affect how you read the text and how you write about it.

1.4 What is analysis?

If your tutor gives you a text and says, 'Analyse that by Tuesday', you will not only have to read it, you will also have to write something. If you compare the text you read with the text you write, you can begin to see what analysis is.

Activity 1.2

Purpose: to begin thinking about the meaning of 'analysis'.

Task: look at Extracts 1.5 and 1.6 in Resource Book 1. One is from a case study and the other is from an analysis of that case study.

1   Which extract is from the case study?
2   Which extract is from the analysis?
3   Why do you think this?

Remember, again, you don't need to understand the extracts fully to do this activity.

Compare your answers with those suggested in the Answer section.

Comment

One extract is from the text that a student reads and the other comes from the text that a student writes. The texts are different because they have different purposes. The process of turning one text into the other is the process of *analysing a business case*.

It is useful to see analysing a business case as a kind of process or **system**. In business studies, the idea of a system is often used to describe a business. For example, a bakery business can be seen as the following system shown in Figure 1.1.

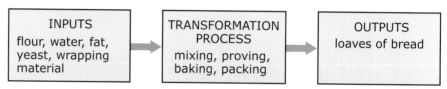

Figure 1.1   The process of producing bread

Doing a business case analysis can be seen in a similar way. A case study is one of the inputs; it is processed by a student who reads, thinks and writes about it; the case analysis is the output or product (Figure 1.2).

Figure 1.2   The process of producing a case study analysis

We should make it clear how the words *case, case study, case analysis* and *analysing a business case* are used in this book. The *case* or the *case study* is the text which a student reads about the case. The *case analysis* is the text which a student writes about the case study. The activity of producing a case analysis is often called *doing a case study*; here it is also called *analysing a business case*.

1.5   Types of input text in business case analysis

There are more input text types than the case study itself. This section introduces some of these other inputs and begins to look at the first part of the analysis process: reading.

Whether you find reading a text easy or difficult depends on how much knowledge you already have about the six features you looked at in Activity 1.1: **content**, **organisation**, **language**, **writer**, **reader** and **purpose**.

The next activity focuses on the first of these features: content.

Mind maps

What makes reading difficult is the number of words in a text and the great variety of ideas. Reading with understanding means that you can reduce all those words and ideas to a few key words or ideas. A good way of doing this is called mind mapping.

Activity 1.3 ....

Purpose: to introduce mind maps and develop your content knowledge for the next reading activity.

Task 1: the visual below represents three of the main ideas from the extracts you are going to read.

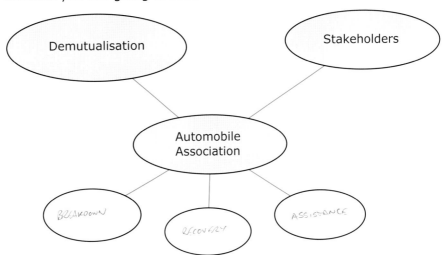

Figure 1.3(a) Mind map of Automobile Association case study

Before you read the text extracts in Activity 1.4, you may already know something about these three ideas. To find out, in the three empty bubbles next to 'Automobile Association', write any words which come to mind when you think of the AA.

Compare your answer with the one suggested in the Answer section.

Comment ....

There are many words which you could connect with 'Automobile Association'. If you belong to the AA or work for it, you will have more knowledge and more words – and reading the texts is likely to be easier. If you live outside the UK and have never heard of the AA, you may have fewer words and reading the texts may be harder.

Task 2: you read the word 'stakeholders' in Activity 1.2. Figure 1.3(b) shows another mind map with empty bubbles. Look at the first two paragraphs of Extract 1.6. Find some words to write in the empty bubbles next to the idea 'stakeholders'. One example has already been done for you.

Compare your answer with the one suggested in the Answer section.

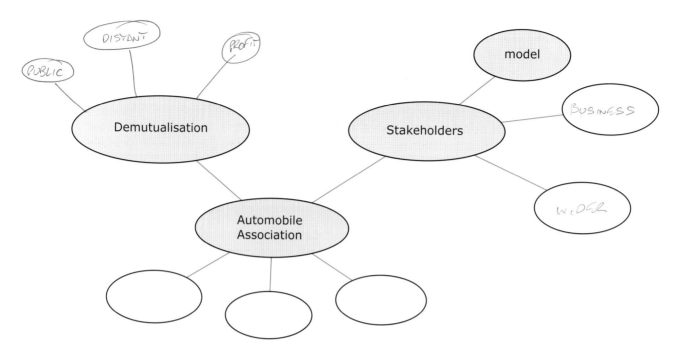

Figure 1.3(b) Mind map for Activity 1.3

Comment ....

Stakeholder is a more specialised word than *Automobile Association*. If you have studied business courses before and know this word, you will find the extracts in Activity 1.4 easier to read. If the idea is new to you, it may be more difficult to read the extracts.

Task 3: the third word in the mind map is *demutualisation*. This is a key word in the texts. Here is some background information on the idea.

> For many years, the AA was a mutual association. This meant that AA was owned by its members. In 1999, the AA began to talk about changing into a Public Limited Company on the Stock Exchange. This process is called demutualisation. The decision was an important one because it could affect members' profits.

Now draw three more bubbles on the mind map next to *demutualisation* and write in some words about demutualisation.

Compare your answer with the one suggested in the Answer section.

Comment ....

Mind maps can be used for different purposes when you are processing a case study text. Drawing a mind map of your knowledge before you read a text is one of the reading strategies you will practise in this session.

In the next activity, the knowledge of *Automobile Association*, *stakeholder* and *demutualisation*, which you have just considered, should help you to read the four extracts more quickly.

Purpose: to identify some other input text types from the process of business case analysis.

Task 1: look at Extracts 1.7 to 1.10 in Resource Book 1. Under each extract there is a table of features. Tick the features which best describe the extract. It is not necessary to read the extracts carefully to do this activity.

Task 2: Table 1.1 lists some texts. Identify which text each extract comes from and write the number of the extract in the column on the right.

Table 1.1 For use with Activity 1.4

Text	Extract number
AA Trust annual report	1.10
AA case study	1.9
Instructions for carrying out a case study assignment	1.7
Business studies textbook explaining the stakeholder framework	1.8

Compare your answers with those suggested in the Answer section.

These are all input texts to read when you analyse a business case. In a systems model of business case analysis, your success depends on your skills in processing these input texts and producing output texts such as the analysis in Activity 1.2. The next section looks more closely at the skills you need for this process.

1.6 Analysing business cases – the six skills

This course breaks down the process of analysing a business case into six main skills.

1 Mapping the case
2 Framing the case
3 Recognising influences and impacts
4 Identifying problems
5 Proposing solutions
6 Evaluating the analysis

Each of these skills is introduced and practised in the six sessions of this book. For now, here is a brief introduction with a short explanation of each skill (see also Figure 1.4).

1 Mapping the case

The first step is to read the case study to get an overview of the situation (covered in this session).

2 Framing the case

Here you read the case study in a different way, using business studies concepts to frame the way you see the case (Session 2).

3 Recognising influences and impacts

At every stage in the case analysis process, the way in which 'one thing leads to another' is central. This is the skill of explaining why events turn out the way they do, or will do in the future (Session 3).

4 Identifying problems

Identifying that certain situations or events are problems and describing them provides the basis for solving them (Session 4).

5 Proposing solutions

Here you identify or create solutions for the problems you have identified (Session 5).

6 Evaluating the analysis

You provide reasons for the particular solutions you prefer, predict how they are likely to work out, express concerns about likely difficulties with the solutions and recommend ways forward. In short, you persuade your reader to accept your analysis (Session 6).

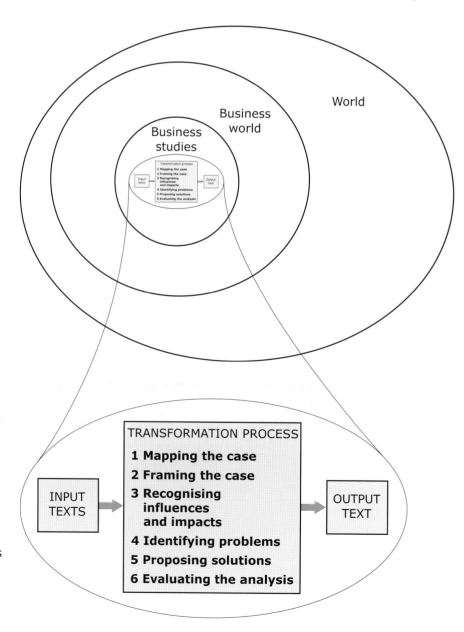

Figure 1.4 The communication skills of analysing a business case: (a) the external environment; (b) the business studies environment

1.7 Mapping the case

For the rest of this session, you will practise the first skill of mapping the case. In the process, you will develop strategies for effective reading and do more work with mind maps. You will practise your skills on a case study text about the airline industry in the USA; so you will develop language for reading and writing about this industry in particular and company performance generally. Finally, you will transfer the skills you have practised to some other case studies and discuss your experiences with other people on the course who are doing this work.

The skill of reading is central to processing a case study text. However, there are different ways of reading. It is quite common to read texts in different ways and you probably already do this.

Activity 1.5

Purpose: to think about whether you have different reading strategies for different texts.

Task: write down some of the texts you read in everyday life. Then think about whether you read them all in the same way or whether you approach them differently. For example, do you read them from beginning to end? Do you read them carefully or not? Do you make notes when you are reading?

Compare your answers with those suggested in the Answer section.

Comment

Your different reading strategies depend on the output you want. If you read a novel for pleasure, you may miss out the parts that you don't enjoy. The output you want affects how you read. On the other hand, when you read a business case study, pleasure is probably not the output you want. Your output is often a text and so the process of reading a case study is different from the novel-reading process.

What you are going to study in this first session is an active reading method.

An active reading strategy

These are the techniques you will practise on the case study text 'US Airlines'. They can be applied to any case study.

- Be clear what output you want from reading the text.
- Before you read carefully, look quickly through the text to see what it is generally about (good places to look are the title, introduction, first sentences of each paragraph and final paragraph).
- Consider what you already know about the case.
- Think of a question that the text will answer **before** you read.
- Keep asking more questions while reading.
- Read the text carefully and try to notice how it is organised.
- Underline **high levels** in the text ('levels' are explained later in this session).
- Write on the text.
- Write notes somewhere else, not on the text, and if possible, draw mind maps.
- Produce a summary.

Be clear what output you want from reading the text

This first technique is important. How you read a text depends on the output you want. Sometimes case studies are given to illustrate an idea in business studies courses. However, the motive for reading 'US Airlines' is to write an analysis. When you have to write an analysis you should first get a general idea of the case. That is what **mapping the case** means. When you have mapped the case, you can move to the actual analysis, which begins in Session 2 with **framing the case**.

So the activities in this session focus on active reading techniques and will result in a summary of the case study.

Before you read carefully, look quickly through the text to see what it is generally about

To practise this reading technique, you will look only at the first three paragraphs.

Activity 1.6

Purpose: to practise looking quickly through a text.

Task: look quickly through the title and first three paragraphs of 'US Airlines' (Text 1.11 in Resource Book 1).

Comment

From this very quick look, you may already have an idea what the case study is about. Only a few words might have stayed in your mind but they are the basis of the next technique.

Think what you already know about the case

As you have seen, the case study you are going to read is called 'US Airlines: big carriers unlikely to find much relief'. You may already understand what the text is about but there are several reasons why the text may not be easy to read. This is why you are going to do some activities to build your knowledge of the content. If you find that the text is easy for you to read, think about how you could use these techniques when you do more difficult reading.

Activity 1.7

Purpose: to focus on the knowledge you already have about the case study 'US Airlines'.

Task: this case study was written two years after the terrorist attack on the World Trade Center in New York. At that time, the US airline industry had some major problems. The title of the case study tells you that the text is about the two ideas in the bubbles in Figure 1.5. Around the bubbles, write down anything you can think of about these two ideas.

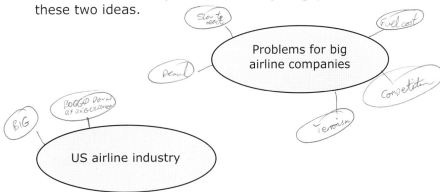

Figure 1.5   For use with Activity 1.7

Compare your answers with those suggested in the Answer section.

Comment

This activity used the technique of mind mapping which was introduced earlier. It is a way of gathering your thoughts about a text you are going to read. As you read, the new knowledge in the text can be connected to the knowledge you already have.

Think of a question that the text will answer for you *before you read*

When you read any text actively, it is good to have a question or two that you hope the text will answer. When you are doing a case study assignment, there will usually be an assignment question. It is a good idea to read the case study before you start thinking about the assignment question. At this stage, you may just have a simple question in mind, such as 'What is this text about?' or you may have a more focused question, such as 'What is the biggest problem for the airline industry?' Think of a question that this text may answer for you.

Read the text carefully

To practise this technique, and to introduce the text, you will read only the first three paragraphs carefully. You will read the rest of the text later.

Activity 1.8 ....

Purpose: to introduce the 'US Airlines' text and practise careful reading and mind mapping.

Task: look at Extract 1.12 in Resource Book 1 which consists of a mind map and a simplified version of the first paragraph of 'US Airlines'. Each sentence in the paragraph is numbered. Match each sentence with an idea in the mind map and write the sentence number next to it.

Repeat this process for Extracts 1.13 and 1.14. This time there may be more than one idea in the mind map that matches each sentence in the extracts.

Compare your answers with those suggested in the Answer section.

Comment ....

Normally, of course, when you are reading a case study, you would not be given a mind map or a simplified text. They are used here to introduce this case study text. However, making a mind map is a good way of making notes on a text.

The previous activity introduced the content of the 'US Airlines' case study by focusing on the first three paragraphs. But it is important to remember that these paragraphs are part of a bigger, whole text. Before you do the next activity, have a quick look back at the complete 'US Airlines' case study, Text 1.11. You will read this whole text closely later in this session. In the next activity you will again focus on the first three paragraphs and the meanings of the words in these paragraphs.

Activity 1.9 ....

Purpose: to read the first three paragraphs of the case study text closely.

Task: Extract 1.15 in Resource Book 1 is from the original case study. Next to the case study text some of the ideas from the text are written in different words. This activity will focus your reading on the meanings of those words. Read the case study text and decide whether the words in the right-hand column mean the same as the words in the case study text. If so, tick them; if not, put a cross as shown below.

For example, many airlines have tightened up existing cabin baggage regulations and have begun to strictly enforce excess baggage charges	tightened up = made stricter ✓ existing ... regulations = out-of-date regulations ✗ strictly enforce = made stricter ✗ excess baggage = extra baggage ✓

Compare your answers with those suggested in the Answer section.

Comment

This activity focused on the process of careful reading. When you are reading difficult texts, it is normal to find words that are hard to understand. However, it is not necessary to understand **all** the words in a text to understand the text. A good reader only has to understand **enough** words.

Good readers use the following techniques when they meet words they don't understand:

- decide whether it is necessary to understand the word
- use their general knowledge of what words mean
- use their general knowledge of the situation which the words are dealing with
- look at other words in the text to see whether they help to understand the words they don't understand
- use a dictionary
- ask someone.

Which technique you use depends on the output you want from the reading. Some people use a dictionary for every word they don't understand. However, it is usually not necessary to understand every word if the output is just a general understanding of the text.

Before you move on to read the rest of the case study, the next activity checks your understanding of the beginning of the text. The beginning of a text is important for understanding what it is about. Try to use your memory of the text or the mind maps in Resource Book 1 to answer the questions and not the actual case study.

Activity 1.10

Purpose: to check your understanding of the first three paragraphs of the case study.

Task: from memory or from looking at the mind maps, write your answers to the following questions.

1   In a few words, what kind of year have business travellers had?

2   In your own words, give one example of a difficult experience for business travellers.

3   What is the general reason why airlines are trying to obtain more money from passengers?

4   Give one example of how airlines are trying to obtain more money.

5   Would you agree there are four main ways in which airlines are trying to improve their profits? In addition to the example that you gave for question 4, what are the main ways?

6   The case study is based on a newspaper report. Newspaper reports are often called 'stories'. Does this seem like the beginning of a story? If so, how do you think the story will continue?

Compare your answers with those suggested in the Answer section.

Comment   ....

This activity draws your attention to three features of a case study text which can be used in active reading.

1   The beginning of a case study text is important. It sets the scene.

2   Case study texts describe general situations and give examples.

3   A case study is often like a story. Stories are often about how a person or an organisation deals with a problem. With stories you can usually ask the question, 'What will happen next?'

So far, you have practised reading techniques on the first three paragraphs of the case study. Now, you will practise them on the rest of the text.

Before you read carefully, look quickly through the text to see what it is generally about

You have already practised this technique on the title and introduction to the text. The next activity demonstrates how the first sentence of each paragraph can be used as part of a reading strategy.

Activity 1.11   ....

Purpose: to see the value of the first sentence in each paragraph.

Task: Extract 1.16 in Resource Book 1 gives the first sentence of each remaining paragraph in 'US Airlines'. The final sentence of paragraph 10 is also included. Each sentence is summarised below. The order of these summaries is mixed up. Write the correct paragraph number next to each summary.

Terrible state of airline industry
Companies cancelling contracts with big carriers
Not first airline crisis
Competition to big carriers from cut-price operators
Cuts in economy fares
Prospects of war with Iraq
Poor prospects for big carriers and business travellers
Likelihood of reduced number of scheduled flights and routes

Compare your answers with those suggested in the Answer section.

Comment   ....

Although the list above only summarises the first sentence of each paragraph, it gives a good overview of the whole text. In fact, there are only five more main ideas in the text which are not included here. This shows that skimming down the first sentence of each paragraph can tell you what the text is about before you read it carefully. These summaries are like the mind maps discussed earlier. They give a framework into which you can fit the new knowledge from the text.

Read the text carefully and try to notice how it is organised

When you are mapping a case, the purpose is to summarise the case study. You are interested in the general situation and less interested in the details. Luckily, there is something about the way a text works which can help you with this. Texts move up and down between high and low levels.[1] You have already seen something of this in the last two activities. The next activity looks more closely at levels.

Activity 1.12 ....

Purpose: to introduce the idea of **levels in a text.**

Task: the following extract is taken from paragraph 6 of 'US Airlines'. You have already seen a summary of the first sentence of this paragraph in the previous activity. The extract below shows how a text moves from a high level to a low level. The high level is information about the general situation. The low level gives particular examples of this general situation.

Read the text carefully. Mark the text to show where you think the information about the **general situation** ends and the **particular examples** begin (there is a word in the text which tells you).

> The success of low cost 'no-frills' carriers in lucrative markets such as California and the east coast has destroyed the traditional carriers' profits on many routes that they once dominated. For example, Southwest Airlines' share of the California market has jumped to more than 60 per cent in the 18 months while United's share has fallen to less than 20 per cent, in part because losses have forced the big carrier to cut back on its flights. Other low-cost airlines, such as Spirit Airlines and Jet Blue, have begun cutting into big carriers' business on longer routes.

Compare your answer with the one suggested in the Answer section.

Comment ....

In this extract the general situation is *low cost 'no-frills' airlines have destroyed the profits of traditional carriers*. The rest of the extract gives examples of this general situation. The text moves from a high-level generalisation to a low-level particular. The words *for example* tell you this.

The levels are shown in Figure 1.6.

When you map the case, the idea is to see the general situation. The high level information gives you this general situation. However, low level particular information is not only examples. It can also be other kinds of detail.

---

[1] The course authors would like to acknowledge Janet Giltrow as the source of these activities on levels in text. The idea is very effectively introduced in her book, *Academic Writing*, 1995, Broadview Press.

High level: general

The success of low-cost 'no-frills' carriers in lucrative markets such as California has destroyed the traditional carriers' profits on many routes

(For example)

Southwest Airlines' share of the California market has jumped...

Low level: particular

Figure 1.6 Levels in a text

Activity 1.13 ....

Purpose: to see other kinds of low-level information in a text.

Task: read the paragraph below carefully and mark the text to show where you think the **general situation** ends and the **particular details** begin. (This time there is a signal word which tells you where the high-level information begins but not where the lower level details begin.)

Overall, the US airline industry is in a terrible financial state. Last year alone, operators lost about $8bn on top of the more than $7bn they lost in 2001. The six biggest carriers – American, United, Delta Air Lines, Northwest Airlines, Continental and US Airways – have all suffered badly. Southwest Airlines was the only significant carrier that did not cut back operations last year and its profitability, amid a sea of losses, has earned it a stock market value bigger than all its rivals combined.

Compare your answer with the one suggested in the Answer section.

Comment ....

The first sentence gives the general idea: *the terrible financial state of the airline industry.* The rest of the paragraph gives particular details about this *terrible financial state.* The word *Overall* in the first sentence signals that this sentence is an <u>overview</u> of the general situation (Figure 1.7).

High level: general

(Overall) the US airline industry is in a terrible financial state

Last year alone, operators lost about US$8bn on top of the more than US$7bn they lost in 2001. The six biggest carriers...

Low level: particular

Figure 1.7 More levels in a text

These sentences, which give a general idea of the situation, are called generalisations. When you can see the high-level generalisations in a text, you have an overview of what the text is about.

There can be more than two levels in a text as the next activity shows.

Activity 1.14

Purpose: to see more than two levels in a paragraph.

Task: in Activity 1.12, you looked at the second half of this paragraph. The high-level generalisation from that activity is underlined below. In the first half of the paragraph there is a generalisation at an even higher level. Underline it.

> But even without an oil price spike, the traditional carriers in the US were already facing fierce competition from cut-price operators such as Southwest Airlines and three-year-old upstart, Jet Blue. Most have acknowledged that they will have to slash costs if they are to survive. <u>The success of low cost 'no-frills' carriers in lucrative markets such as California and the east coast has destroyed the traditional carriers' profits on many routes that they once dominated.</u> [...]

Compare your answer with the one suggested in the Answer section.

Comment

The higher-level generalisation in this paragraph is

> the traditional carriers in the US were already facing fierce competition from cut-price operators.

It is more general than the sentence you underlined in Activity 1.12:

> The success of low cost 'no-frills' carriers in lucrative markets such as California ...

Both sentences deal with **competition between traditional carriers and cut-price operators in the USA** but the first sentence deals with competition generally. The second sentence looks at competition *in lucrative markets such as California and the east coast*. The levels are shown in Figure 1.8.

High level: general

Competition between traditional carriers and cut-price operators in the USA

The success of low-cost 'no-frills' carriers in lucrative markets such as California

Southwest Airlines' share of the California market

Low level: particular

Figure 1.8   Three levels in a text

A successful reader is able to see the levels in a text. Often, **the high-level generalisation is the first sentence of a paragraph**. This is why the first sentences of each paragraph in Activity 1.12 give an overview of the whole case study.

Similarly, the first paragraph of a text often gives a good idea of what the rest of the text is about.

The levels in the first paragraph of 'US Airlines' are shown visually in Figure 1.9.

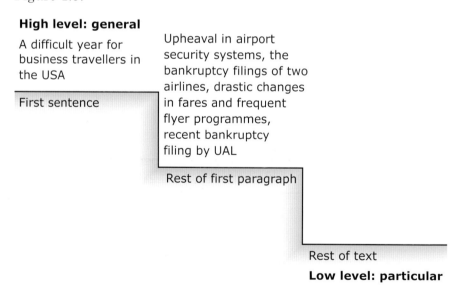

High level: general

A difficult year for business travellers in the USA

First sentence

Upheaval in airport security systems, the bankruptcy filings of two airlines, drastic changes in fares and frequent flyer programmes, recent bankruptcy filing by UAL

Rest of first paragraph

Rest of text

Low level: particular

Figure 1.9   Levels in the first paragraph

Activity 1.15 ....

Purpose: to practise identifying high-level generalisations in the text.

Task: Text 1.17 in Resource Book 1 is the complete version of the case study 'US Airlines'. The high-level generalisations in the first six paragraphs are already underlined. (Ignore the notes for the moment.)

1 Read through the first six paragraphs carefully to see whether you agree that these are the high-level generalisations.

2 Underline the high-level generalisations in the last four paragraphs.

Compare your answers with those suggested in the Answer section.

Comment ....

For paragraphs 9 and 10 you might have underlined almost the whole paragraph. Note making is a decision-making process and you may decide that underlining an entire paragraph is necessary to map the general meaning of the text. Paragraph 10 is the final paragraph, which often summarises all of the text, so it is difficult to leave much of this out.

To make notes you also have to find a way of reducing the information to fewer words. You will look at this note-making technique next.

Write notes and, if possible, draw mind maps

If you copied out all the high-level generalisations underlined in Text 1.17, you could produce a short summary. However, you could produce a more useful summary if you reduced these generalisations to fewer words. You have already seen some examples of these in Activity 1.10. You matched short word groups to the first sentence of each paragraph. These short word groups are not sentences but they communicate most of the meaning of the sentence they summarise. Here are the notes for the first paragraph.

Case study text	Notes
It has been a difficult year for business travellers in the US. Over the past 12 months US business travellers have been forced to put up with upheaval in airport security systems in the wake of the September 11th (2001) terrorist attacks, the bankruptcy filings of two big airlines, and drastic changes in fares and frequent flyer programmes. The recent bankruptcy filingby UAL, the Chicago-based parent of United Airlines, the world's second largest carrier, is likely to add to the uncertainty.	difficulties for US business travellers upheaval in airport security after terrorist attacks two airline bankruptcies drastic changes in fares and frequent flyer programmes UAL bankruptcy

In the notes, the original words

> It has been a difficult year for business travellers in the US

have been reduced to

difficulties for US business travellers

> Over the past 12 months US business travellers have been forced to put up with upheaval in airport security systems in the wake of the September 11th (2001) terrorist attacks

have been reduced to

upheaval in airport security after terrorist attacks

Each of these short word groups is a key idea or a key concept from the case study. If you can reduce the case study text to a few key concepts like this, your notes will be a **map of the case**. In the next activity you can practise doing this.

Activity 1.16 ···

Purpose: to look at how key concepts can be used to map the case.

Task: look at Text 1.17. In the notes column, key concepts are written next to the generalisations they summarise. However, some key concepts are missing. They are listed below in a mixed-up order. Write each one in the notes column next to the part of the text they summarise.

additional charge for same-day standby flights
cost slashing by big carriers
cut-price competition
internet shopping-around
increases in business fares
tightened cabin bag regulations
terrorist fear
restrictions to frequent flyer programmes
likelihood of reduced number of schedules flights and routes

Compare your answers with those suggested in the Answer section.

Comment ···

Producing key concepts like these is a powerful way of reducing text to make notes. There are other ways of reducing sentences. For example, the two sentences below can be reduced by leaving out the underlined words.

> the traditional carriers in the US were already facing fierce competition from cut-price operators. Most have acknowledged that they will have to slash costs if they are to survive.

The notes would be this shortened sentence:

traditional carriers facing fierce competition from cut-price operators and most acknowledge must slash costs to survive.

However, the key concepts in Activity 1.16 are more useful than shortened sentences. The next section looks at the reason why.

1.8 Nouns and verbs in business case analysis

The discussion about **text** pointed out that words don't work on their own. They work in combination with other words to make larger units of language. The single word *airlines* is a small unit of language. The whole 'US Airlines' text is a large unit of language. In order to process the individual words *airlines*, *fee*, *additional*, *an*, *passengers*, *tickets*, and so on, you have to combine these words together into larger units – they don't work on their own. There are six units of language that are larger than a single word, as follows.

Unit	Example
Word group	*an additional fee*
Clause	*Other airlines have begun to charge an additional fee of up to $25*
Sentence	*Other airlines have begun to charge an additional fee of up to $25 if passengers insist on using paper tickets instead of electronic ones*
Paragraph	All of the words in paragraph 3
Section	This text is not divided into sections but many texts are
Text	All of the 'US Airlines' text

It is useful to know something about these units of language to help you develop professional communication skills. So far, you have worked with *sentences*, *paragraphs* and *texts*. In this section, which looks at note making, you will concentrate on *single words*, *word groups* and *sentences*.

Writing notes means turning a larger unit of language (**a sentence or clause**) into a smaller unit (**a word or group of words**).

First, you will look at some grammar by considering some of the words which make a sentence.

Sentences are made up of nouns and verbs. For example:

> The government deregulated the industry.
>
>   noun   verb   noun

The next two activities look at how nouns and verbs relate to note making.

Activity 1.17 ···

Purpose: to recognise nouns.

Task: nouns are words that name things. Some things are physical, for example: *aeroplane*, *passengers*, *the US*. These are concrete nouns. Some things are not physical but mental; for example: *fear*, *bankruptcy*, *success*. These are abstract nouns.

Look at the list of nouns below. Write 'C' next to the noun if it is concrete and 'A' if it is abstract.

travellers	business	sophistication	the markets	survival
competition	the east coast	Southwest Airlines	terrorist attack	market share
the government	prices	tickets	recession	money
factor	willingness			

Compare your answers with those suggested in the Answer section.

Comment ....

Whether a noun names a physical thing or an abstract thing, they are all **things** – and are different from verbs.

Activity 1.18 ....

Purpose: to recognise verbs.

Task: in the list below, write 'N' for **noun** next to the words or word groups that name a thing. Write 'V' for **verb** next to the words or word groups that are actions or activities.

has destroyed	frequent-flyer programmes	are harassing	complain
the shaky health	have tightened up	airlines	have been charged
insist on	the economic boom	warn	carrier
designed	the prospect of war	have suffered	to squeeze
have to cut back			

Compare your answers with those suggested in the Answer section.

Comment ....

A sentence always has at least one noun and one verb. However, when you are making notes, it is good to reduce sentences to nouns for two reasons.

1 Nouns, particularly abstract nouns, can contain a large amount of information. Think how much meaning there is in the abstract nouns *business*, *competition*, *bankruptcy* or *recession*. You can summarise a whole sentence or paragraph with the noun *competition*, for example. Abstract nouns are ideal for reducing the high-level generalisations in a text to a few words.

2 Nouns can be combined with other words to make **noun groups**. Most of the notes you wrote in Activity 1.16 are noun groups, for example:

additional charge for same-day standby flights

cost slashing by big carriers

cut-price competition

internet shopping-around

increases in business fares.

There is always a main noun in a noun group. The main nouns are underlined above. The other words are combined with this main noun to make the noun group. These combinations are very useful in note making, and in writing generally.

Purpose: to recognise the difference between a sentence and a noun group and identify the main noun in a noun group.

Task 1: below are word combinations taken from the 'US Airlines' text and from the notes. Write 'S' next to the word combinations that are sentences and 'NG' next to those that are noun groups.

Task 2: underline the word which you think is the main noun in the noun groups.

1   Most have acknowledged that they will have to slash costs if they are to survive.

2   Many airlines have tightened up existing cabin baggage regulations.

3   Competition for big carriers from cut-price operators

4   US passengers also face the prospect of fewer scheduled flights.

5   Likelihood of reduced number of scheduled flights and routes

6   Other airlines have begun to charge an additional fee of up to $25 if passengers insist on using paper tickets instead of electronic ones.

7   Charge for paper tickets

8   Tightened cabin bag regulations

Compare your answers with those suggested in the Answer section.

Comment

The focus in this session is on noun groups. Session 2 deals with sentences in more detail.

The next three activities look at how some of the key concepts in the notes on 'US Airlines' were made by reducing sentences to noun groups.

1.9 Creating key concepts

There are three main ways to produce key concept word groups like the ones in the 'US Airlines' notes.

1   Find the key concept in the text.

2   Combine words from the text.

3   Make up the key concept yourself.

Find the key concept in the text

Activity 1.20 ....

Purpose: to practise finding the key concept in the input text.

Task 1: the high-level generalisation in the paragraph below is the highlighted part of the first sentence. There is a key concept in this sentence which represents the whole paragraph. Underline this key concept.

Task 2: All the remaining sentences give further details about the key concept you have underlined in the first sentence. These details are various activities or events that have happened recently in the airline industry. The key concept summarises these activities or events. Underline each of the verbs in the remaining sentences which tell you what activities or events have happened. The verbs in the second sentence have been underlined as examples.

Task 3: *have acknowledged* is underlined as a verb in sentence 2. However, it refers to a different kind of activity or event to the other verbs. What is different about it?

But even without an oil price spike, **the traditional carriers in the US were already facing fierce competition from cut-price operators such as Southwest Airlines and three-year-old upstart, Jet Blue**. Most <u>have acknowledged</u> that they <u>will have to slash</u> costs if they <u>are to survive</u>. The success of low cost 'no-frills' carriers in lucrative markets such as California and the east coast has destroyed the traditional carriers' profits on many routes that they once dominated. For example, Southwest Airlines' share of the California market has jumped to more than 60 per cent in the 18 months while United's share has fallen to less than 20 per cent, in part because losses have forced the big carrier to cut back on its flights. Other low-cost airlines, such as Spirit Airlines and Jet Blue, have begun cutting into big carriers' business on longer routes.

Compare your answers with those suggested in the Answer section.

Comment ....

The key concept in the first sentence generalises about the activities or events in the paragraph by using an abstract noun to name them. In this case, the text already contains a useful abstract noun that the notemaker can use.

Combine words from the text

Activity 1.21 ....

Purpose: to practise putting words together from the input text.

Task: you might decide that the concept identified in Activity 1.16 is too abstract and too general. You may think it is important to make it clearer **what kind** of competition this is and **who** is involved in it. What words from the opening sentence could be combined with *competition* to do this?

Compare your answer with the one suggested in the Answer section.

Comment ....

This is still a key concept, but it is less general than *competition* on its own. To make this a more focused key concept, you have to decide which words to combine with the abstract idea, *competition*, and how to combine them.

Make up the key concept yourself

Activity 1.22   ....

Purpose: to practise making up the words for the key concept yourself.

Task: the sentence below refers to something that is causing problems for the big carriers. Underneath the sentence there are three noun groups. Choose the group which best summarises what is causing problems for the big carriers.

> At the same time, the internet has made it much easier for both business and leisure travellers to compare prices and tinker with itineraries in order to save money.

price comparison	internet shopping-around	money saving

Compare your answer with the one suggested in the Answer section.

Comment   ....

The best words for the concept in this sentence are not in the original text so you have to choose words from outside the text to summarise the sentence.

So there are three main ways of creating the key concepts which you need for making notes on a case study text. This is the process called 'mapping the case'. Look at the notes for the first three paragraphs of Text 1.17. How have the concepts been created?

1.10 Summarising the case

You don't need to read every case study with the same care as you have read 'US Airlines'. It depends on the output you want to produce, how difficult the text is, your reading skills, and how much time you have. Mapping a case is only the first step in analysing a business case study. In this first session you concentrated on the wide range of active reading skills involved in that first step because they are not just important for mapping a case study. They are also relevant to all the later steps in analysing a case.

There are several things you can do with the key concepts created in this process. Now that you have a mental map of the case study, you could move straight to the next step which is **framing the case**. Or you could produce a mind map of the case on paper or on computer using the kind of mind map diagram you saw in Activities 1.3 and 1.4. For longer case studies, you may decide to produce a summary.

The final activity using the 'US Airlines' text is to look at a summary of the whole text. When you write an analysis of the case, you have to turn notes back into sentences and paragraphs. This summary shows how the noun groups in the notes can be turned back into sentences in a paragraph.

Activity 1.23 ....

Purpose: to see how notes based on high-level generalisations and key concepts are used to produce a summary.

Task: in the summary text below, each paragraph in Text 1.17 has been reduced to one or two sentences. Compare the summary with Text 1.17 and, in the summary, identify the sentences which summarise paragraph 1. Mark the text to show where the summary of paragraph 1 ends. Then write P2 for the second paragraph. Make a second mark to show where the summary of paragraph 2 ends. Continue to the end of the summary. Paragraphs 1 and 2 have already been done. There is no summary for paragraph 7.

Summary

[P1] This year has seen serious disturbances for business travellers; these include terrorist-induced upheavals in airport security, two airline bankruptcies, drastic changes in fares and frequent flyer programmes, and a recent bankruptcy in UAL. / [P2] Business passengers are complaining about airline harassment as a result of the industry's worst ever downturn. Examples include: stringent cabin baggage regulations and increased charges / additional charges for paper tickets rather than electronic ones, additional charge for same day standby flights, and restrictions to frequent-flyer programmes. There have also been reductions in the number of scheduled flights. Prospects of war with Iraq threatens an oil price rise and more bankruptcies. Big airlines are suffering from competition by cut-price operators leading to cost slashing by airlines. These cuts in economy fares are being subsidised by increases in business fares. As a result companies are cancelling their contracts with big airlines and using the internet to shop around. This is not the first air-industry crisis but the combination of terrorist fear, cut price competition and internet shopping around is exacerbating it. Prospects are poor for big airlines and business travellers.

Compare your answers with those suggested in the Answer section.

The writer did not look back at the original text to produce this summary. Their key concept notes were enough. At this point they were ready to move into analysing the case. You will do this in Session 2.

1.11 Vocabulary activity

See the Course Guide for how to do a vocabulary-building activity for this session.

1.12 Critical reflection

These questions are for you to reflect on in your Learning Journal.

1   What is your previous experience of business studies?

2   What is your own prior experience of business case analysis? In the past, what have you found difficult and easy about it? If you do not have any experience, what do you expect it to be like?

3   Did you find the 'US Airlines' text easy or difficult to read? Can you explain this? How did it compare with other reading you do?

4   Were the processes you practised in this session similar to your own methods of reading/note making/summarising? How?

5   Have you any experience of reading the other kinds of input texts for case study analysis that you looked at in Activity 1.4?

6   Have you studied grammar, language, or communication before? What are your views on these subjects?

1.13 Review

In this session you have:

- practised mapping a case
- focused on the nature of the input text – the case study
- practised active reading techniques for processing a case (see Section 1.7 for a list of these)
- produced output notes and a summary
- begun to study the grammar of sentences and noun groups.

1.14 Answer section

Activity 1.1

Content	Organisation	Language	Writer	Reader	Purpose
Extract 1.1					
Person	Story	Informal	Lecturer	Student	Education
Extract 1.2					
Organisation	Description	Formal Impersonal	Lecturer	Student	Education

Extract 1.3 (This extract is from a newspaper article written by a journalist. The full text of the article is reprinted as Text 1.18 in Resource Book 1.)

Content	Organisation	Language	Writer	Reader	Purpose
Industry	Story	Informal Personal	Journalist	Public	Entertainment Information

Extract 1.4 (This extract is from a case study written by a lecturer but based on a newspaper article)

Content	Organisation	Language	Writer	Reader	Purpose
Industry	Story	Formal Impersonal	Lecturer Journalist	Student Public	Education Information

Activity 1.2

1 Extract 1.5 is part of <u>a case study text</u> written by a tutor.

2 Extract 1.6 is <u>a case study analysis</u> written by a student.

3 Extract 1.5 is written as a story of the events in the company. It is organised in a sequence with words such as *In the early 1990s, By the end of the decade*. Extract 1.6 is a description organised into groups (types of stakeholders; levels of power).

Activity 1.3

Task 1: car repairs, yellow vans, road maps, car insurance, membership.

Task 2: person, group, affected by activities, cast of players, categories, framework for analysis, wider environment.

Task 3: mutual association, members, share of the profits, public limited company, the stock exchange.

Activity 1.4

Task 1

Content	Organisation	Language	Writer	Reader	Purpose
Extract 1.7					
Person	Description	Formal	Lecturer	Student	Education
Organisation	Explanation	Impersonal			
Extract 1.8					
Organisation	Story	Formal	Lecturer	Student	Education
		Impersonal			Information
Extract 1.9					
Assignment	Explanation	Formal	Lecturer	Student	Education
	Instruction	Impersonal			Information
Extract 1.10					
Person	Story	Formal	Business person	Public	Information
Organisation		Impersonal			

Task 2

Text	Extract number
AA Trust annual report	1.10
AA case study	1.8
Instructions for carrying out a case study assignment	1.9
Business studies textbook explaining the stakeholder framework	1.7

Activity 1.5

You may adopt the following reading strategies for different texts.

Newspapers: you may read them selectively, choosing the stories or the sections of the paper you are particularly interested in.

Magazines: you may flick through them in a waiting room or read them carefully because they deal with topics you are particularly interested in. You may look at the pictures more than the words.

Novels: you may read them to relax. You may start at the beginning, read very quickly or leave out the bits that are boring. You might look at the last page to see what happens.

Websites: you may very quickly search for key words or links to other web pages. You look for pictures, sound or video more than words. You may move between websites and the search engine. You may print out sections.

Mobile phone text: you may read a whole screen in one go or move between texts using the key pad.

Reports: you may use headings to help you move around the report. You may look for summaries, diagrams and conclusions.

Academic writing: you may select what you want to study by looking at the contents page. You may read some sections very carefully and make notes on them or write in the margin of the book.

Activity 1.7

Figure 1.10 shows some of the words you might have written.

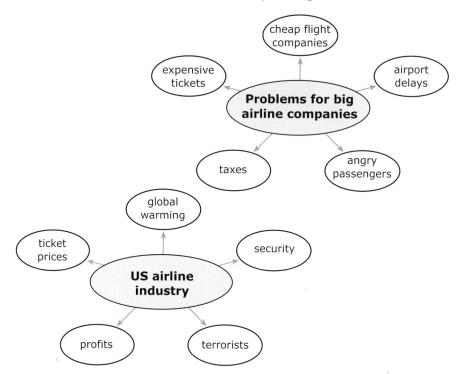

Figure 1.10   Answer to Activity 1.7

Activity 1.8

Extract 1.12

1   difficulties for US business travellers
2   increased security
3   two airline bankruptcies
4   enormous changes in fares and frequent-flyer programmes
5   UAL bankruptcy

Extract 1.13

1   passenger complaints, airline companies, not giving free gifts
2   fighting to survive in bad economic period
3   increased baggage regulations, always charge passengers for too much baggage
4   want more income
5   angry
6   newspaper stories about hundreds of dollars for extra bag
7   business passengers say they pay a high price for poor service

Extract 1.14

1   $25 fee for paper tickets rather than internet, airline companies
2   $100 if standby flight same day as scheduled flight

3   bankruptcy announcements, passengers' fear of losing frequent-flyer miles
4   reduced frequent-flyer programmes but stopped because of criticism

Activity 1.9

Text	Notes
difficult year for business travellers = business has been bad in the USA	✗ If business was bad, business travellers might have a difficult year, but then the opening sentence would probably say 'business' not 'business travellers'.
forced to put up with = had to accept	✓ 'Put up with' means 'accept'.
airport security systems = locks on airport doors	✗ Locks are one kind of security system but airport security is more than door locks.
in the wake of = because of	✗ = after the event, or as an after-effect.
bankruptcy filings = official registration by company that it has no money	✓ = A company can register that it is bankrupt in a court as a way of starting to solve the problem.
drastic = unwelcome	✗ = serious or critical
How many difficulties? = four	? Three difficulties but the third one has two parts.
Chicago-based parent = person who lives in Chicago	✗ 'Parent company' is a kind of company, not a person: the main company in a group.
is likely to add to the uncertainty = uncertain whether the situation will get worse	✗ The situation is uncertain and is likely to get more uncertain.
Many = many airlines	✗ = many people or passengers
fighting for survival = passengers fighting for survival	✗ = the airlines are fighting for survival
one of the industry's worst-ever downturns = airline industry's worsening performance	✓
are harassing them = passengers complaining about airlines	✗ = the airlines are causing difficulties for passengers.
measures designed to squeeze additional revenues out of passengers = actions intended to get more money from passengers	✓
tightened up = made stricter	✓
existing regulations = out-of-date regulations	✗ = regulations that already exist.

strictly enforce = made stricter	✗ = used more strictly.
excess baggage = extra baggage	? = baggage which is extra to permitted amount.
moves = actions	✓
acquire additional revenues = obtain extra income	✓
run the risk of alienating passengers = might send passengers overseas	✗ = make passengers feel angry and hostile towards the airlines.
featured = focused on	✓
charged hundreds of dollars = asked to pay hundreds of dollars	✓
premium prices = top prices	✓
not reflected in standards of service = services are not top quality	✓
charge an additional fee = passengers pay more for electronic tickets than paper ones	✗ = passengers pay more for paper tickets than electronic ones
they reversed themselves a few weeks ago = they introduced the charge a few weeks ago	✗ = they stopped the charge a few weeks ago.
fly standby = fly in an alternative or substitute plane	✓
scheduled flight = cancelled flight = it is more expensive to fly standby on the same day as the original scheduled flight	✓
the bankruptcy filings have left millions wondering whether their frequent-flyer miles are safe = passengers are worried about airline safety	✗ = passengers are worried that they will lose the free bonus miles they get for flying many times with the same airline.
restrictions to frequent flyer programmes = limitations to the special services they offer to passengers who use planes frequently	✓
forced to back down in the face of a barrage of criticism from customers = made to change their minds by the strong objections from passengers	✓

Activity 1.10

1   A very difficult, disturbed and alienating year.
2   Having to pay extremely high excess baggage charges.
3   They are in the middle of an economic downturn in the industry.
4   Reducing frequent-flyer programmes.
5   Yes: additional fee for paper tickets; charge if travelling same day on a standby flight; high excess baggage charges; reduced frequent-flyer programmes.
6   Yes: more of the same bad experiences; no happy ending in sight.

Activity 1.11

[P4] Likelihood of reduced number of scheduled flights and routes
[P5] Prospects of war with Iraq lead to oil price rise and more bankruptcies
[P6] Competition to big carriers from cut-price operators
[P7] Terrible state of airline industry
[P8] Cuts in economy fares
[P9] Companies cancelling contracts with big carriers
[P10] Not first airline crisis
[P10 end]
Poor prospects for big carriers and business travellers

Activity 1.12

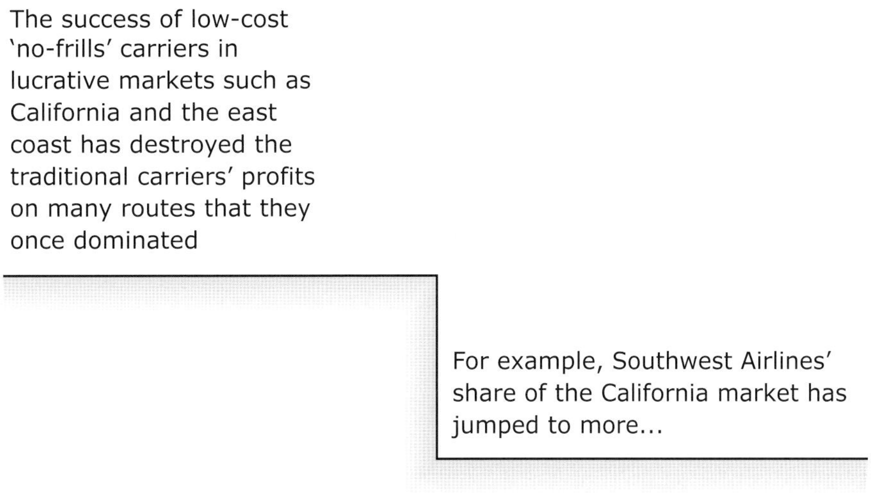

The success of low-cost 'no-frills' carriers in lucrative markets such as California and the east coast has destroyed the traditional carriers' profits on many routes that they once dominated

For example, Southwest Airlines' share of the California market has jumped to more...

Figure 1.11   Answer to Activity 1.12

Activity 1.13

Overall, the US airline
industry is in a terrible
financial state

Last year alone, operators lost
about US$8bn on top of the more
than US$7bn they lost in 2001

Figure 1.12   Answer to Activity 1.13

Activity 1.14

But even without an oil price spike, the traditional carriers in the US were already facing fierce competition from cut-price operators such as Southwest Airlines and three-year-old upstart, Jet Blue.

Activity 1.15

Paragraph 7

Overall, the US airline industry is in a terrible financial state.

Paragraph 8

most carriers have been forced to cut their already heavily discounted economy fares further.

most big carriers have raised prices for last minute bookings and business fares.

Paragraph 9

prompted many companies to re-examine their business travel policies, cancel trips and in some cases abandon the deals they had previously negotiated with big carriers. At the same time, the internet has made it much easier for both business and leisure travellers to compare prices and tinker with itineraries in order to save money.

Paragraph 10

This is not the first time the US airline industry has been plunged into financial turmoil.
But the combination of the fear created by September 2001 terrorist attacks, competition from cut-price airlines and the growing sophistication of travellers who now have access to comparative fare information via the internet makes this downturn different, say analysts. With the continuing uncertainty over the US economic recovery and geopolitics, the big carriers are unlikely to find much relief this year. For business travellers, that may translate into further uncertainty and turmoil.

Activity 1.16

[P2]	tightened cabin bag regulations
[P3]	additional charge for same-day standby flights; restrictions to frequent-flyer programmes
[P4]	likelihood of reduced number of scheduled flights and routes
[P6]	cost slashing by big carriers
[P8]	increases in business fares
[P9]	internet shopping-around
[P10]	terrorist fear, cut-price competition, internet shopping-around

Activity 1.17

travellers	C	business	A	sophistication	A	the markets	A	survival	A
competition	A	the east coast	C	Southwest Airlines	C	terrorist attack	C	market share	A
the government	A	prices	A	tickets	A	money	C	factor	A
willingness	A	recession	A						

Activity 1.18

has destroyed	V	Frequent-flyer programmes	N	are harassing	V	complain	V
the shaky health	N	have tightened up	V	airlines	N	have been charged	V
insist on	V	the economic boom	N	warn	V	carrier	N
designed	V	the prospect of war	N	have suffered	V	to squeeze	V
have to cut back	V						

Activity 1.19

Task 1: 1 = S; 2 = S; 3 = NG; 4 = S; 5 = NG; 6 = S; 7 = NG; 8 = NG.

Task 2: 3 = competition; 5 = flights; 7 = charge; 8 = regulations.

Activity 1.20

Task 1

competition

Task 2

have acknowledged, will have to slash, are to survive, has destroyed, dominated, has jumped, has fallen, have forced … to cut back, have begun cutting.

Task 3

All the other verbs tell us about the activities or events in the 'competition'. *Acknowledge* does not give more information about the competition itself but shows that the traditional companies are aware of what is happening.

Activity 1.21

Fierce competition **between the traditional carriers and the cut-price operators**.

Activity 1.22

internet shopping-around

Activity 1.23

Summary

[P1] This year has seen serious disturbances … and a recent bankruptcy in UAL. /

[P2] Business passengers … and increased charges, /

[P3] additional charges … frequent-flyer programmes. /

[P4] There have also been reductions … of scheduled flights. /

[P5] Prospects of war … and more bankruptcies. /

[P6] Big airlines are suffering … cost slashing by airlines. /

[P8] Cuts in economy fares … increases in business fares. /

[P9] As a result companies … the internet to shop around. /

[P10] This is not the first … business travellers. /

SESSION 2 Framing the case

2.1 Introduction

In Session 1 you mapped a case but the reading strategies you used were not especially **business** studies strategies. You could read texts on many subjects in the same way you read 'US Airlines'. In contrast, the skill called **framing the case** in this session is definitely a business studies reading strategy. When you frame a case you read it using key concepts from business studies. By using these business studies concepts you can move from reading to analysing.

This session uses two reading strategies from the study reading method in addition to the ones practised in Session 1.

- Think of a question that the text is going to answer for you **before** you read.
- Keep asking more questions during reading.

There is a great range of business concepts and questions you can use to frame a case. In this session, the concepts and questions which are used come from two analytical frameworks: STEP and stakeholder analysis. These frameworks have been chosen because they are good examples of how business concepts organise the way you read a case.

Learning outcomes

In this session, you will:

- develop the skills of reading a case with an analytical framework in mind

- work with the concepts from the STEP and stakeholder frameworks
- look at output texts which are framed by these frameworks
- learn more about sentences and word groups
- use some business studies concepts to write a case analysis.

2.2 Framing a case with a STEP framework

A good example of an output text organised by business studies concepts is a STEP analysis (Figure 2.1).

Figure 2.1   The STEP analysis process

Processing an assignment title

The assignment title gives you the questions to ask when you read a case study. Here is an example of an assignment question about STEP analysis.

> **Carry out a STEP analysis outlining the main factors in the external environment influencing the US airlines industry.**

The assignment title tells you what output text to produce and frames the way you read the input text. It usually does this by giving you an instruction and some of the key concepts you should use.

Activity 2.1

Purpose: to introduce a method for processing an assignment question. To develop your understanding of the STEP analysis framework.

Task: using two different colours, underline the instruction and the key concepts in the assignment question above.

Compare your answer with the one suggested in the Answer section.

Comment

This method of underlining the instructions and the key concepts is useful for any assignment question. It means that you won't arrive at the end of a long case study analysis to discover that you followed the wrong instruction or framed the case using the wrong concepts.

Activity 2.2

Purpose: to practise identifying instructions and key concepts in case study assignment questions.

Task: underline the key concepts in the five assignment questions below. Draw a circle around the instructions. Please note: you don't have to understand the concepts to do this activity.

1   Use the stakeholder model of business environments to examine critically the external environment of Asda–Wal-Mart as outlined in the Case Study.

2   The changes in Potts Garden Centre business appear to be based on a move from one type of business structure to another. Describe the two types of structure using appropriate concepts. Then write about the problems and benefits of moving from one structure to another.

3   Wal-Mart is a US-based multinational corporation. Critically discuss the likely costs and benefits of its takeover of Asda, a UK-based company.

4   Gap takes great care in its vendor selection process, but still receives criticism for the working conditions in some of its suppliers. Outline the key aspects of a vendor selection and monitoring process that will serve Gap's long-term best interests.

5   Compare and contrast Gap's staff management policy with its outsourcing policy.

Compare your answers with those suggested in the Answer section.

Comment ....

Each of the concepts in these titles is a conceptual framework to frame your reading of the case study. For example, the second assignment asks you to use the concept *business structure.*

Processing a textbook text

Teaching business concepts is the purpose of another input text – a textbook. A good example of a business concept in the 'US Airlines' STEP assignment is *external environment. Environment* is a word in everyday use but in business studies it has a specialised meaning, as the next activity shows.

Activity 2.3 ....

Purpose: reading to understand a business concept.

Task: read extract A below which is from a business studies textbook and answer this question: 'What does *external environment* mean?'

> ### *Extract A*
>
> The term 'environment' in this case refers to much more than the ecological, 'green' issues that the word commonly evokes. 'Environment' here is more appropriately interpreted as the external context in which organisations find themselves undertaking their activities. Each organisation has a unique external environment that has unique impacts on the organisation, due to the fact that organisations are located in different places and are involved in different business activities, with different products, services, customers, and so on. (Capon, 2004:278)

Compare your answer with the one suggested in the Answer section.

Comment

Defining concepts

Paragraphs such as this which define key concepts are common in business studies writing. How is this one organised? It starts with a high-level generalisation.

Activity 2.4

Purpose: to look at how the paragraph on *external environment* is organised.

Task: use Figure 2.2 to summarise each sentence in the paragraph. If possible, reduce each sentence to a noun group.

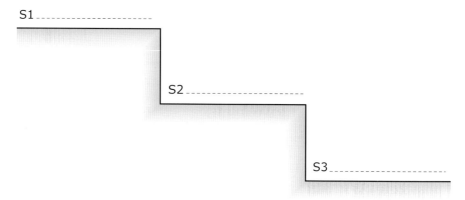

S1 _____

S2 _____

S3 _____

Figure 2.2   For use with Activity 2.4

Compare your answers with those suggested in the Answer section.

Comment

This paragraph shows that everyday meanings are not business meanings. The paragraph starts with a word from everyday life. It then moves down a level to show what the same word means in business studies. Then it gives more details about the business meaning of the word.

Definition paragraphs use **definition words**:

term, refers to, commonly evokes, more appropriately interpreted as.

Textbooks define business concepts carefully. Students are expected to do the same in their assignments. The next activity involves some more examples of how business studies textbooks define *environment*.

Activity 2.5 ....

Purpose: to look at how textbooks introduce a key concept.

Task: read Extracts 2.1 to 2.5 in Resource Book 1. They all introduce the concept *environment*. You will need different coloured pens for this activity.

1(a) Which two extracts directly **define** what the word *environment* means?

  (b) Underline some definition words. (Some examples are underlined in Extract 2.1.)

2(a) Which three extracts do not discuss the meaning but **describe** the environment and how it interacts with business?

  (b) Underline some language needed to describe the way business and environment interact. (Some examples are underlined in Extract 2.4.)

3(a) Which two extracts classify environments into **types** or categories of environment?

  (b) Use a different coloured pen to underline some classification language.

4(a) Which two extracts **describe the composition** of the environment?

  (b) Use a different coloured pen to underline some language of composition.

5   Which extract highlights the word environment with

        italics – *environment*

        inverted commas – 'environment'

        bold type – **environment**.

6   Choose **one or two** of the word groups below to summarise each extract.

interdependency	categories of factors	everything outside the business
external context	environmental impacts on the organisation	types of influence

Compare your answers with those suggested in the Answer section.

Comment ....

When textbooks introduce a concept they discuss what it means, how it works or what it does, and what it is composed of. These are also the ways you can introduce the concepts you use to frame an assignment.

Introducing concepts

Activity 2.6 ....

Purpose: to practise introducing a concept which frames a case.

Task 1: write a paragraph introducing the concept *environment*, based on the noun groups you chose in question 6 in Activity 2.5.

Task 2: read Extracts 2.6 to 2.8 in Resource Book 1 which are from students' assignments. Compare how they introduce the concept *environment* with the way you have. Did they write about what it means, how it works, what it does, or what it is composed of?

Compare your answers with those suggested in the Answer section.

Comment ....

The grammar of definition sentences

To write definitions, you can use six kinds of sentence. In Session 1 you looked at this sentence:

> The government *deregulated* the industry in 1978.
>
>   noun   verb   noun

The verb is an action word, so this is an **action sentence**. Some definition sentences are action sentences. For example:

1   action sentences

> Businesses operate in different environments.

However, not all verbs are actions. There are five other kinds of sentence for defining concepts, as follows.

2   being sentences

> 'Environment' is the external context in which organisations operate.

3   having sentences

> Each organisation has a unique external environment.

4   meaning sentences

> The term 'environment' refers to more than ecological, 'green' issues.

5   reporting sentences

> Lucas suggests that environment is 'a set of external conditions under which a business operates'.

6   existence sentences

> There are three kinds of environment.

Look back at your paragraph in Activity 2.6. Which kinds of sentence did you use?

The STEP framework

Here is the assignment question again.

Carry out a <u>STEP analysis</u> outlining the <u>main factors</u> in the <u>external environment</u> <u>influencing</u> the <u>US airlines industry.</u>

The main concept – or set of concepts – is the STEP framework. If you have studied this framework before, this assignment instruction will make sense. In case you haven't, the next activity introduces the STEP framework. It shows that it is based on four key concepts which you use to frame the case. These concepts are different from the ones you created in Session 1. When you analyse a case using the STEP framework, the concepts you use come from outside the case. You use the STEP concepts to turn the case from a story into an analysis.

Activity 2.7 ···

Purpose: to relate the four high-level concepts of a STEP framework to the details they frame.

Task: Text 2.9 in Resource Book 1 explains the four concepts which make up a STEP analysis. They are: **social, technological, economic** and **political influences**. Each paragraph gives details about one of these concepts. Write the correct heading for each paragraph in the gap at the beginning of the paragraph.

Compare your answers with those suggested in the Answer section.

Comment ···

You might not have needed to read all the words in this text to do this task. The four key concept words can be placed in the correct gap as soon as you recognise **one or two** details in the paragraph. Each general concept is the central word of a mind map with many other concepts. Figure 2.3 is the mind map from the text for **political influences**.

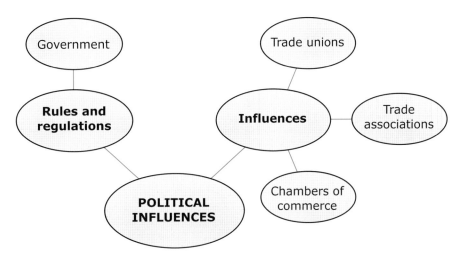

Figure 2.3 For use with Activity 2.7

This is a limited mind map and there are many other concepts which could be included under **political influences** but, like all mind maps, this is a starting point.

Influences and impacts

There is a third concept in the assignment title which must frame the case study analysis. All the social, technological, economic or political influences must be *factors* which *influence* the US airline industry. There is a difference between a political *event* or *situation* and a political *factor*.

Activity 2.8 ....

Purpose: to contrast *factor* with *event* or *situation*.

Task: extract B below gives some information about an economic situation. Which part of the situation is a factor which influences Nike?

> *Extract B*
>
> Nike's presence in emerging countries can have an enormous economic impact on them. China is now the biggest shoe-producing country in the world; Nike is Vietnam's biggest employer. Jobs are scarce and people want to work for companies such as Nike and Reebok.

Compare your answer with the one suggested in the Answer section.

Comment ....

There is a difference between the information framed by the concept *economic events* or *situation*, and the information framed by the concept *economic factors*.

In summary, for an event to fit the economic category in a STEP analysis, the criteria are that it is (i) **economic**, (ii) in the **external environment** and (iii) a **factor influencing the industry**.

If you read a case with business concepts such as this in mind, you are **framing the case**.

2.3 A student's STEP analysis of 'US Airlines' – the texts

Activity 2.9 ....

Purpose: to see how business concepts organise the information in a STEP analysis.

Task 1: Text A below is a student's STEP analysis of the 'US Airlines' case (Text 1.11 in Resource Book 1). Read the text below and underline each factor in the analysis.

Task 2: look at Text 1.11 in Resource Book 1 and use a coloured pen or highlighter to mark the events which have been included as factors in the student's text. Write S, T, E or P in the margin, to show whether the event is categorised as a social, technological, economic or political factor.

When you have completed these two tasks, answer the questions in Task 3 at the end of the STEP analysis.

Text A

Carry out a STEP analysis outlining the main factors in the external environment influencing the US airline industry.

Introduction

All successful businesses must react and adapt to the environments in which they operate. Businesses have to be able to recognize the environments within which they operate and be able to identify those elements that may have the greatest effects upon them. There are a number of models available to assist a business in identifying these. One of these is the STEP analysis. This divides the operating environment of a business into four areas, Social, Technological, Economic and Political. This analysis will use the STEP framework to outline the various influences shown to affect the business operation in the case study 'US airlines: big carriers unlikely to find much relief'.

STEP Analysis

As stated by Armson et al. (1995, p. 12) the advantage of the STEP framework is its simplicity and applicability in analyzing current and continuing influences on organizations. It is evident from the case study that there are a number of different influences that impact on both US airline carriers and their passengers.

The specific focus of this analysis will be the 'traditional' carriers, those airlines that charge full fares and offer in-flight services. This is in contrast with the 'cut-price' operators who charge much lower fares and in turn offer reduced services for customers. It is the traditional carriers that are suffering the worst effects from the environmental factors discussed below.

Social

One social factor demonstrated in the case study that has had an impact on the airline business is the underlying downward trend in passenger air travel. A second social factor that has had an impact on existing carriers has been the willingness of the travelling public to use the services of new low-cost carriers. This has required a social change in terms of people becoming willing to accept a lower level of service than they had been used to. Moreover the willingness of travellers to use new technology (particularly the internet) in order to find the lowest cost travel products has meant that airlines have been forced to compete on price.

Technological

Major developments in technology, particularly in the use of the internet by both business and leisure passengers, have enabled travelers to compare prices between airlines and book their own tickets selecting the most cost-effective route and itinerary. This has forced airlines to be more competitive in their pricing. Technology has also enabled airlines to reduce their overheads in issuing tickets through the use of internet booking systems which enable passengers to be supplied with electronic tickets instead of paper ones. This has allowed airlines to charge an additional fee if passengers request a paper ticket and so technology has enabled the airlines to keep down their costs.

Economic

As stated in the case study, a number of economic factors have affected the airline industry. Some of these include the significant increase and success of cut-price and no-frills airline operators giving the traveller greater options when considering which carrier to use. This in turn has forced the traditional carriers to review their pricing structure and their routes, and to consider other ways of increasing revenue such as cutting back on frequent flyer points. The fact that large airlines have filed for bankruptcy has had an unsettling effect on the industry in general and has caused widespread financial uncertainty.

Whilst the threat of a war with Iraq could be seen as a political factor, it does have a major economic impact upon both the airline industry and its passengers. The threat of war could cause a significant rise in oil prices which would further add to the economic pressure on the industry whilst the potential rise in ticket costs could add to the downturn in airline passenger traffic.

Political

The main political factors affecting the health of the airline industry are the terrorist attacks of September 11th 2001 and the threat of similar attacks in the future which have made passengers more reluctant to travel. As mentioned above, the possibility of war with Iraq has caused concerns because this would lead to an increase in oil prices. In the past, political factors that had a negative impact on the industry included deregulation in 1978, and the recessions of the 1980s and 1990s. This time, however, the situation is more complex and there is a wider set of issues at work.

Conclusion

It is evident from the case study that by carrying out a STEP analysis an organisation is able to give consideration to the many possible factors that may have an impact on its current and future health.

Task 3: the following questions focus on differences in the organisation of the case study text (1.11) and the analysis (above).

(a) Compare the first paragraphs of the two texts. Which of the noun groups below is the best summary for each paragraph?

social factors	STEP framework	US airlines
difficult year for business travellers	environments	

(b) In the input text, there is a lot of information about low-cost companies. Why doesn't the student analyse the environmental factors influencing these organisations?

(c) In the analysis, all the social factors are in one paragraph, the technological factors in a different paragraph, and so on. Is this true for the case study? Why?

(d) Does the case study use the words *social* or *technological*?

(e) How does the student know which events are social or technological?

(f) Does the case study use the words *economic* or *political* every time it refers to an economic or a political event?

(g) How does the student know an event is economic or political?

(h) According to the student, which events in the case study are:

political <u>and</u> economic

technological <u>and</u> economic

technological <u>and</u> social?

(i) In the case study, there is a lot of information about the problems of passengers. Is this information included in the STEP analysis? Can you explain this?

Compare your answers with those suggested in the Answer section.

Comment ....

The case study and the analysis are organised differently because they have different purposes. The order of the events in the case study is changed; the events in the story are treated as *factors influencing the organisation*; and the events are categorised as *social*, *technological*, *economic* or *political*. In this way, the STEP analysis brings a new understanding to the case study.

The next section looks at how the student produced this analysis.

2.4 A student's STEP analysis of 'US Airlines' – the process

In Session 1, you used active reading strategies to get an overview of the case study but when you read to analyse it, you are **searching** for information. This kind of reading can be called search-reading.

There are two strategies from the active reading method which are particularly important in search reading:

- think of a question that the text is going to answer for you before you read
- keep asking more questions during reading.

When you search-read for a STEP analysis you are reading with the following questions in mind.

Is this event economic (or social, or political, or technological)?

Is it in the external environment?

Does it influence the big airline companies?

It is also important to make notes actively when you search-read. It is best when making notes for a STEP analysis to use a STEP analysis table, as the next activity shows.

Activity 2.10 ....

Purpose: to practise making notes for a STEP analysis.

Task 1: the noun groups below are factors from the 'US Airlines' case. Write each factor in the appropriate category in the blank STEP analysis table.

uncertain geopolitics	newspaper articles
use of e-tickets	government deregulation
downturn in passenger traffic	use of internet to obtain best fares
willingness to use low-cost flights	war with Iraq
threat of terrorism	willingness to use internet
cabin baggage regulations to enforce excess baggage fees	recession

Social	*Technical*
Economic	*Political*

Purpose: to practise active search reading and note making.

Task 2: no economic factors are included in the list above. Search-read Text 1.11 looking for economic factors. Use the following questions.

> Is this event economic?
>
> Is it in the external environment?
>
> Does it influence the big carriers?

Transfer the economic factors to the STEP table, reducing the sentences to word groups.

Task 3: are there any factors included in the STEP table which shouldn't be there because they are not *in the external environment*?

Compare your answers with those suggested in the Answer section.

Comment ....

Like all reading, it is easier to do the search-reading process in Task 2 if you already know something about the concepts and language of the text. However, for a STEP analysis you use a mind map of concepts which are not in the text but are in your mind. The economic concepts from the text which you looked at in Activity 2.7 include: *the impact of banks*, *stock markets*, *the world money markets*, and *trading blocs such as the European Union*.

If these were all the economic concepts you had in mind when you read 'US Airlines', you would not find any economic factors. None of these are mentioned. However, if your mind map for *economic influences* includes concepts such as *rise in oil prices*, *airlines filing for bankruptcy* and *recession*, you will be able to frame these events using a STEP framework. This is why business studies courses stress the importance of key concepts. Business studies involve a process of learning which concepts to use and how these concepts are understood by other people.

2.5 The language of STEP analysis

Sentences become word groups

Most of the factors the student wrote in the STEP analysis table were abstract noun groups such as *government deregulation, potential rise in oil prices* and *use of e-tickets*.

As suggested before, abstract nouns are useful in note making because they reduce generalisations to fewer words.

Activity 2.11 ....

Purpose: to see how STEP factors are sentences turned into word groups.

Task: below there are six word groups used in the STEP table and six extracts from the 'US Airlines' case study text. For each extract write down the word group that summarises it.

Word groups

(a) use of internet to obtain best fares

(b) use of e-tickets

(c) threat of terrorism

(d) willingness to use low-cost flights

(e) government deregulation

(f) potential rise in oil prices

Extracts from 'US Airlines'

(i)   Since the government deregulated the industry in 1978, it has faced two serious recessions in the early 1980s and 1990s.

(ii) ... the increasingly likely prospect of a war with Iraq could cause oil prices to spike, further undermining the shaky health of many US airlines and leading to the possibility that other carriers could go bust.

(iii) Other airlines have begun to charge an additional fee of up to $25 if passengers insist on using paper tickets instead of electronic ones.

(iv) At the same time, the internet has made it much easier for both business and leisure travellers to compare prices and tinker with itineraries in order to save money.

(v)   the combination of the fear created by September 2001 terrorist attacks ... makes this downturn different, say analysts

(vi) the traditional carriers in the US were already facing fierce competition from cut-price operators such as Southwest Airlines and three-year-old upstart, Jet Blue. Most have acknowledged that they will have to slash costs if they are to survive. The success of low cost 'no-frills' carriers in lucrative markets such as California and the east coast has destroyed the traditional carriers' profits on many routes that they once dominated. For example, Southwest Airlines' share of the California market has jumped to more than 60 per cent in the 18 months while United's share has fallen to less than 20 per cent.

Compare your answers with those suggested in the Answer section.

Comment ....

As discussed before, abstract nouns such as *deregulation*, *rise* and *threat* are concepts packed with meaning. They can also be combined with other words such as *government*, *potential*, *oil prices* and *terrorism* to include even more meaning.

Abstract nouns turn actions into things

When the student did the STEP analysis, she focused on the **events** and **actions** that affected US airlines. But when she wrote these into a STEP category in the table she usually wrote them as **noun** groups rather than **verb** groups. As you know, nouns are words for things. By using a noun for an event or an action instead of a verb, you make it more like a thing. In analysis writing this is useful; the following activities show how this can be done.

Activity 2.12 ....

Purpose: to see how actions are turned into things.

Task: the sentences below are from the 'US Airlines' case. The verbs in each sentence are underlined. After each sentence there is the noun group which the student wrote as a factor in the STEP table. For each factor, decide whether the student (i) found the noun group in the sentence, (ii) adapted it from words in the sentence, or (iii) created it herself.

(a) Since the government <u>deregulated</u> the industry in 1978, it has faced two serious recessions in the early 1980s and 1990s.

government deregulation

(b) the increasingly likely prospect of a war with Iraq <u>could cause</u> oil prices <u>to spike</u>, further undermining the shaky health of many US airlines and leading to the possibility that other carriers could go bust.

potential rise in oil prices

(c) Other airlines <u>have begun to charge</u> an additional fee of up to $25 if passengers <u>insist on using</u> paper tickets instead of electronic ones.

use of e-tickets

(d) At the same time, the internet <u>has made it much easier</u> for both business and leisure travellers <u>to compare</u> prices and <u>tinker</u> with itineraries in order <u>to save</u> money.

use of internet to obtain best fares

(e) ... the combination of the fear created by September 2001 terrorist attacks ... <u>makes</u> this downturn different, say analysts.

threat of terrorism

Compare your answers with those suggested in the Answer section.

Comment ....
When actions are turned into things they are easier to categorise in the STEP analysis table.

Activity 2.13 ....

Purpose: to practise turning actions into things.

Task: Extract 2.10 in Resource Book 1 contains extracts from four different case studies. Reduce each extract to a noun group which could be an environmental factor in a STEP analysis. Identify whether it is a social (S), technological (T), economic (E) or political (P) factor.

Compare your answers with those suggested in the Answer section.

Factors which are nouns can influence businesses

The first stage in a STEP analysis is to identify STEP factors and organise them into groups. The second stage is to write an analysis which shows how these factors influence businesses.

When processes are turned into nouns, it is much easier to show how they influence businesses. If you look at the grammar again, you can see why.

Sentences must have at least one noun and one verb, for example:

Vodafone paid £6 billion to the government.

noun   verb   noun   noun

However, one noun and one verb do not necessarily make a sentence, for example:

paid £6 billion

verb   noun

The reason this is not a sentence is because the noun – *£6 billion* – is not the subject of the verb.

Vodafone paid £6 billion is a sentence because the verb has a subject, the noun *Vodafone*. In other words, there is something (*Vodafone*) which does the action (*paid*).

When **factors** are turned into nouns in STEP analysis they can also be the subjects of verbs. When factors are subjects of verbs they can do actions; and the main action they can do is **influence organisations**.

Activity 2.14 ....

Purpose: to note how factors which are nouns can be subjects and do actions.

Task: the sentences below are from the student's STEP analysis. They have been slightly shortened for this activity. Underline the factor in each sentence. Then circle the main verb which says how the factor influences the industry.

(a) A significant rise in oil prices would further add to the economic pressure on the industry.

(b) The use of the internet by both business and leisure passengers has enabled travelers to compare prices between airlines and select the most cost-effective route and itinerary.

(c) The terrorist attacks of September 11th 2001 and the threat of similar attacks in the future have made passengers more reluctant to travel.

(d) The use of internet booking systems has also enabled airlines to reduce their overheads.

Compare your answers with those suggested in the Answer section.

Comment

When events and actions in the case study are turned into things, they can be used in sentences which describe how these events influence an organisation. And that is the purpose of a STEP analysis.

Activity 2.15

Purpose: to write a short STEP analysis.

Task 1: read Extract 2.11, 'Nike and the vexed issue of corporate responsibility', in Resource Book 1 and use a STEP analysis table to frame your notes. Use the search-reading and note-making methods you have practised in this session. Extract 2.11 does not include information for all the STEP categories. Then write the analysis. In your introduction you should make it clear which categories your analysis deals with.

Task 2: at the end of this session there is a Reflection page which lists the skills and knowledge covered so far. When you have finished this activity, use the Reflection page to help you write a reflection on it in your Learning Journal.

Task 3: compare your notes and written analysis with the example analysis which will be published on the course website.

Activity 2.16

Purpose: to practise framing a difficult case study using a STEP analysis framework.

Task 1: Text 2.12, 'The growth of CCTV systems', in Resource Book 1 is not an easy text. So, it is a good text for practising the active reading method. First, map the case well using the active reading strategies introduced in Session 1. Then use a STEP table to frame your reading of the case and make notes, using the strategies you have practised in this session. Use the Reflection page at the end of this session to guide you in this task. You do not need to write up the notes as a full analysis.

Task 2: compare your notes with the example STEP analysis notes at the end of Text 2.12 in Resource Book 1.

Task 3: use the Reflection page to review the process of writing this analysis. Write your reflections in your Learning Journal.

2.6 Stakeholder analysis – a different set of concepts

STEP analysis is a categorising framework so it is easy to see how STEP concepts are used to frame a case. However, **framing the case** can be done using any business studies concept. Throughout this course you will practise framing cases with various other concepts.

For the rest of this session you will look at a conceptual framework called stakeholder analysis. This also categorises information about the environment of a business. However, the concept questions that are used to organise stakeholder information are:

>   Does this organisation or person have an interest in the business?

>   Does this organisation or person have power in relation to the business?

The two concepts framing this analysis are *power* and *interest*.

Activity 2.17 ....

Purpose: to introduce the concepts *power* and *interest*.

Task: read extracts C and D below. Which one can be summarised by the word *power* and which can be summarised by the word *interest*?

> ### Extract C
>
> Many individuals, groups and organisations are likely to be affected by the strategic decisions that a business makes. As a result of these decisions, employees may have to work harder, undertake new tasks, or face the prospect of leaving the company. Shareholders in the company, banks which have loaned the organisation money, governments concerned about employment will be watching company performance closely. Customers and suppliers will also be involved in different ways.
>
> ### Extract D
>
> In different types of organisation, different stakeholder groups have a dominant position. Commercial organisations are either shareholder-led or dominated by directors and senior managers. The views of both of these groups are important for the direction of the organisation. Service industries are usually customer-led. Co-operatives tend to be member-led.

Compare your answers with those suggested in the Answer section.

Comment ....

The abstract nouns *power* and *interest* are both important concepts in business studies. One way of defining them is to use them in a sentence. Here is an example using the noun groups, *high power* and *high interest*.

Stakeholders with high power are those who can do most to affect the organisation.

Stakeholders with high interest are those who will be most affected by the actions that the organisation does.

Analysing a business case using the stakeholder framework follows the same general process as STEP analysis (Figure 2.4).

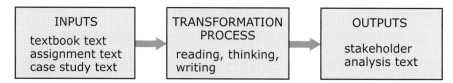

Figure 2.4   The process of writing a stakeholder analysis

There are several different stakeholder frameworks in business studies but they are all generally based on the concepts of *power* and *interest*. The one introduced in the next activity creates a set of four categories using these concepts.

Activity 2.18 ....

Purpose: to learn the categories in a stakeholder analysis framework and to practise some active reading strategies on a textbook text.

Task 1: look quickly at Text 2.13, 'Analysing stakeholders', in Resource Book 1 to get an impression of what it is about and how it is organised.

Task 2: Figure 2.5 is called a 'matrix diagram'. It is referred to in the first paragraph of Text 2.13. Read this paragraph and write in the four missing words on the diagram.

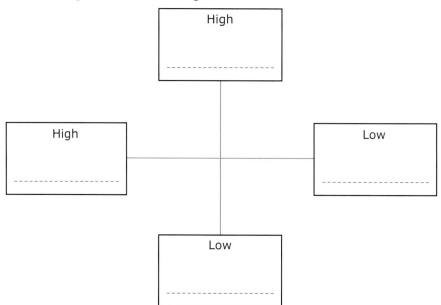

Figure 2.5   Stakeholder matrix diagram

Task 3: search-read Text 2.13 to find **some examples** of stakeholders. Write these into the empty bubbles in Figure 2.6. Two are filled in for you already.

Figure 2.6 The stakeholders in an organisation

Compare your answers with those suggested in the Answer section.

Figures 2.5 and 2.6 show how the concepts of power and interest can be used to organise individuals and groups into stakeholder categories.

Next you will look at a stakeholder analysis assignment with the following title:

> **Use the stakeholder model of the business environment to analyse the main influences on the Automobile Association during its demutualisation process.**

The case study for this assignment is Text 2.14 in Resource Book 1.

Activity 2.19

Purpose: to practise framing an analysis using the concepts *stakeholder*, *power* and *interest*.

Task: Extract 2.15 in Resource Book 1 is from an analysis text with the title above. The original text was organised using the categories you have just read about. However, in Extract 2.15, the sections of the text are mixed up. The section headings, the categories and the words *high* and *low* have been removed from the text. Read the text and decide where the following headings should go.

Stakeholders with high power and high interest (category D)

Stakeholders with high power and low interest (category C)

Stakeholders with low power and high interest (category B)

Stakeholders with low power and low interest (category A)

Compare your answers with those suggested in the Answer section.

Comment

To produce an analysis, the writer reorganised the structure of the case study text. The original text has a story structure with time sequence words organising the events (*By 1990*, *During the 1990s*, and so on). The new structure is organised into categories using the key concept words *power* and *interest* and categorising words such as *category*.

In Activity 2.19, you had to find evidence in the text to decide where to put the headings. This is what a case analysis writer does when analysing a case study. To put a particular stakeholder in a category, the writer has to judge the stakeholder's level of power and interest.

Activity 2.20

Purpose: to focus on how the 'AA stakeholder analysis' uses evidence from the case to categorise stakeholders.

Task 1: look at Text 2.16 in Resource Book 1. For each stakeholder, highlight the sentences or words which tell you which **category** the stakeholder belongs to and write C in the notes column. Then underline the sentences or words which give the <u>reason</u> why the particular stakeholder belongs in this category and write R in the notes column.

Here is an example from the first paragraph.

John Maxwell and his management team were key players with high power and high interest	C
<u>as their planning and decision making would determine their future with the AA, the future of the AA, the future of those who worked for the AA, and the future of AA members.</u>	<u>R</u>

Task 2: in the notes column, write down:

(a) whether the evidence for the category comes from the case study (Text 2.14) or from the writer's general business knowledge

(b) whether the reason is an example of the *power* or the *interest* of the stakeholder, or both.

Compare your answers with those suggested in the Answer section.

Comment

Each time a group of stakeholders is categorised, the analyst gives particular examples of their *power* or *interest* to show why they belong in this category. This means the analysis moves up and down between high-level generalisations (*power* and *interest*) and low-level details (examples of power and interest). The paragraphs begin with a general statement about the stakeholder and their power and interest and then moves down to particular details which show their power and interest in action.

The writer can use three kinds of evidence to decide which category a stakeholder belongs in.

1   The case study text may say directly how much power or interest a stakeholder has.

2   The stakeholder's actions or the organisation's actions may show who has power or interest.

3   The person analysing the case study may have general business knowledge that helps them decide.

Categorising

Stakeholder and STEP analysis reorganise information from the case study. This basic process of reorganising is called **categorising**. These two frameworks were chosen because they are particularly strong examples of categorising in business case analysis. They show how business analysis groups people, organisations, situations or events according to particular criteria. As long as you know the criteria and can judge whether a particular person, organisation, situation or event fits the criteria, you are able to categorise. This applies to any business concept. Some concepts are bigger categories than others. *Marketing*, for example, is a bigger category than *competition* or *segmentation*. Some are more precise and formal than others. *Relative cost position*, for example, is more precise and formal than *profitability* or *entrepreneurship*. However, all these concepts are used in business studies to generalise about large amounts of business detail – particular people, organisations, situations or events.

Formal categories, such as *types of environment*, can be set up using formal categorising language. Extract 2.5 in Activity 2.5 uses this kind of language as follows.

The environment <u>consists</u> of many <u>elements</u>.	**items to be categorised**
These elements can be <u>classified</u> <u>into two categories</u>	**categorising process**
<u>depending on</u> the level of influence they have on the business.	**criterion for categories**
One is the *operating environment* <u>which is composed of</u> ...	**a category**
... <u>elements</u> that the business can influence and which influence the business.	**members of one category**
The other is the *remote environment* <u>which is composed of</u> ...	**another category**
... <u>elements</u> that the business cannot influence but which influence the business	**members of another category**

Categories can be set up with less formal definitions. For example, this is a definition of the *social environment*:

> The social environment is concerned with people's needs, wants and aspirations – with lifestyle and with the shapers of markets

(Finlay, 2000, p. 211)

However, to use any business concept to frame an analysis of a case study, you need to understand the general area it covers so you can fit the details from the case study into it.

2.7 A different stakeholder framework

The text in the next activity was produced by a student who read a slightly different input text about the stakeholder framework. As a result she framed the case slightly differently. The case study she read is too long to present here but Extract 2.11 in Resource Book 1 is one page from it.

*Application
Activity 2.21*   ....

Purpose: to compare the framing of two stakeholder analyses.

Task: Text 2.17 in Resource Book 1 is a student's stakeholder analysis of a case study about Nike (see Extract 2.11 for part of this case study). The stakeholder model the student uses is slightly different from the one you have been studying but they are both based on the concepts of *power* and *interest*. Compare the organisation and structure of Text 2.17 and Text 2.16 and make notes on the differences and similarities in your Learning Journal. Also, identify any language which you think is used to frame the case and justify the categorising.

2.8 Vocabulary activity

See the course website for the vocabulary-building activity for this session.

2.9 Critical reflection

By the end of this session you should have developed the skills and knowledge which are listed on the Reflection pages. In your Learning Journal review how far your skills and knowledge have developed during this session and write a reflection in your Learning Journal.

2.10 Review

After studying this session, you should have:

- developed the skill of reading a case with an analytical framework in mind
- developed your understanding of the concepts from the STEP and stakeholder frameworks
- developed the skills of writing an analysis framed by business concepts
- learned more about sentences and word groups.

Reflection

Analysing business cases

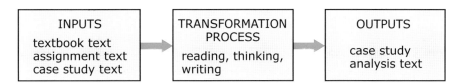

Figure 2.7 The process of writing a case study analysis

Communication skills

1   Be clear why you are reading the text.

Processing input texts – mapping

(a) Read the case study text to map the case.
1   Before you read closely, look quickly through the text to see what it is about.
2   Ask yourself questions about the text.
3   Read the text carefully.
4   Underline high levels in the text.

(b) Process the case study text by making notes.
1   Select information, using levels in the text to decide.
2   Make or find key concepts for the levels.
3   Organise the key concepts into notes.

(c) Produce a summary
1   Produce a summary (in your head, in writing or in a diagram).

Processing input texts – framing

1   Read the assignment title and identify instructions and concepts.
2   Read textbook texts and develop concept knowledge.
3   Search-read and make notes on the case study to frame the case with business concepts.

Producing an analysis text

1   Define the concepts you are using.
2   Organise the analysis.
3   Provide criteria for categories.
4   Give examples and details for categories.
5   Use evidence from the case study or elsewhere as rationale for analysis.

Language knowledge

How texts are organised
• Case study: story, description
• Case analysis: concepts

- Levels in text:
    high-level generalisations and key concepts
    low-level: examples and details

How texts are structured
- First paragraphs
- First sentences of paragraphs

How sentences are structured
- Nouns and verbs
- Subject and verb

How word groups are structured
- Noun groups

Business studies knowledge
- STEP concepts:
    external environment
    social, technological, economic, political factors
- Stakeholder concepts: power, interest
- US airline industry
- Automobile Association demutualisation
- CCTV industry
- Nike

2.11 Answer section

Activity 2.1

The instruction is: *Carry out a STEP analysis outlining ...*

The key concepts are: (i) the STEP framework; (ii) the *external environment*; (iii) *factors ... influencing*; (iv) *the US airline industry*.

Activity 2.2

The key concepts are in **bold** and the instructions are underlined.

1 <u>Use the</u> **stakeholder model** of **business environments** <u>to examine critically</u> the **external environment** of **Asda–Wal-Mart** as outlined in the Case Study.

2 **The changes in Potts Garden Centre** business appear to be based on a **move from one type of business structure to another**. <u>Describe</u> **the two types of structure** <u>using appropriate concepts</u>. Then <u>write about the</u> **problems and benefits** of **moving from one structure to another**.

3 **Wal-Mart** is **a US-based multinational corporation**. <u>Critically discuss</u> the likely **costs and benefits** of its **takeover of Asda, a UK-based company**.

4 **Gap** takes great care in its **vendor selection process**, but still receives **criticism for the working conditions in some of its suppliers**. <u>Outline</u> **the key aspects** of a **vendor selection and monitoring process** that will serve **Gap's long-term best interests**.

5 <u>Compare and contrast</u> **Gap's staff management policy** with its **outsourcing policy**.

Activity 2.3

External environment means the *external context*.

Activity 2.4

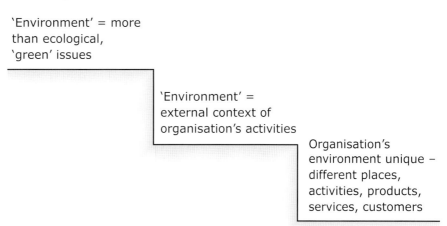

'Environment' = more than ecological, 'green' issues

'Environment' = external context of organisation's activities

Organisation's environment unique – different places, activities, products, services, customers

Figure 2.8   Answer to Activity 2.3

Activity 2.5

1(a) Extracts 2.1 and 2.2

(b) Extract 2.1

The term

refers to much more than

the word commonly evokes.

is more appropriately interpreted as

Extract 2.2

the term

has taken on a rather specialised meaning

it involves 'green'

we use the term 'the environment' in a much broader sense to describe

This includes

2(a) Extracts 2.3, 2.4 and 2.5

(b) Extract 2.3

Figure 3–1 suggests the interrelationship between the firm and its remote, its industry, and its operating environments.

In combination, these factors form the basis of the opportunities and threats that a firm faces in its competitive environment.

Extract 2.4

the interdependence between a business organisation and the environment within which it operates

society depends on business organisations for most of the products and services it needs,

Conversely, business organisations depend on society for the resources they need.

Business organisations are not self sufficient, nor are they self-contained.

are dependent upon the environment in which they operate. Business organisations and society, depend on each other.

This mutual dependence entails a complex relationship between the two.

This relationship increases in complexity when certain variables in the environment, such as technological innovation, economic events or political developments, bring about change in the environment which impacts in different ways on the business organisation.

Extract 2.5

First, there is the *operating environment,* composed of elements that the organisation can influence and that also influence the business.

Second there is the *remote environment,* composed of elements on which the individual business has no significant influence but which may have a major effect on the operating environment and on the business.

3(a) Extracts 2.3 and 2.5

(b) Extract 2.3

can be divided into three interrelated subcategories: factors in the *remote* environment, factors in the *industry* environment, and factors in the *operating* environment.

Extract 2.5

The elements in the external environment can be classified by the level of influence that they have on the business and the business has on them. As a result a business can be considered to have two environments, depending the direction of the influences between the business and the elements within them. First, there is the *operating environment*, composed of elements that the organisation can influence and that also influence the business. Second there is the *remote environment,* composed of elements on which the individual business has no significant influence but which may have a major effect on the operating environment and on the business.

4(a) Extracts 2.2 and 2.5 (and possibly 2.3)

(b) Extract 2.2

the term 'the environment' ... includes customers, competitors, suppliers, distributors, government and social institutions.

Extract 2.3

These factors which constitute the *external environment*

Extract 2.5

composed of elements

5   Using italics – *environment*   Extracts 2.3 and 2.5
    Using inverted commas – 'environment'   Extracts 2.1 and 2.2
    Using bold type – **environment**   None

6   Extract 2.1   **external context** and **environmental impacts on organisation**

Extract 2.2   **everything outside the business**

Extract 2.3   **categories of factors and interdependency**

Extract 2.4   **Interdependency**

Extract 2.5   **environmental impacts on the organisation** and **types of influence**

Activity 2.6

Task 1 (my example paragraph)

The environment of a business is composed of all the factors that influence the business. There is an interdependency between the environment and the business, with the business influencing the environment and the environment influencing the business. Factors can be classified according to whether they are in the near environment or the far environment. Factors in the near environment are more under the control of the business than factors in the far environment.

Task 2

My paragraph does not use any meaning sentences; Extract 2.6 does but the other extracts do not. My paragraph looks at the interaction between the environment and the business. Extract 2.7 does the same. Extract 2.8 also talks about the level of control that a business has over the near and far environment like my paragraph. My paragraph classifies environments in the same way as Extract 2.6. Extract 2.8 classifies environments using the STEP model (or framework).

Activity 2.7

The correct headings are political, economic, social, technological.

Activity 2.8

The economic factor influencing Nike is that jobs are scarce in these countries. The information that Nike is having an economic impact on the country is a factor influencing the country not Nike.

Activity 2.9

Task 1 (underlined) and Task 2

Social
the underlying trend of the downturn in passenger air travel.

Many are now complaining that airlines, fighting for survival in the midst of one of the industry's worst-ever downturns

Faced with the success of the low price carriers and the underlying downturn in passenger traffic,

the willingness of the travelling public to use the services of new low-cost carriers.

The success of low cost 'no-frills' carriers in lucrative markets such as California and the east coast has destroyed the traditional carriers' profits on many routes that they once dominated.

Moreover the willingness of travellers to use new technology (the Internet)

At the same time, the internet has made it much easier for both business and leisure travellers to compare prices and tinker with itineraries in order to save money.

Technological
in the use of the internet

At the same time, the internet has made it much easier for both business and leisure travellers to compare prices and tinker with itineraries in order to save money.

issuing tickets by the use internet booking systems

Other airlines have begun to charge an additional fee of up to $25 if passengers insist on using paper tickets instead of electronic ones.

Economic

<u>the significant increase and success of cut price and no frills airline operators</u>

The success of low cost 'no-frills' carriers in lucrative markets such as California and the east coast has destroyed the traditional carriers' profits on many routes that they once dominated.

<u>the threat of a war with Iraq</u>

<u>rise in oil prices</u>

A more immediate concern is that the increasingly likely prospect of a war with Iraq could cause oil prices to spike,

Political

<u>the terrorist attacks of September 11th 2001 and the threat of similar attacks in the future</u>

upheaval in airport security systems in the wake of the September 11th (2001) terrorist attacks

But the combination of the fear created by September 2001 terrorist attacks,

<u>the possibility of war with Iraq</u>

A more immediate concern is that the increasingly likely prospect of a war with Iraq

<u>deregulation in 1978</u>, and <u>the recessions of the 1980s and 1990s</u>.

Since the government deregulated the industry in 1978, it has faced two serious recessions in the early 1980s and 1990s.

<u>a wider set of issues at work.</u>

But the combination of the fear created by September 2001 terrorist attacks, competition from cut price airlines and the growing sophistication of travellers who now have access to comparative fare information via the Internet makes this downturn different, say analysts. With the continuing uncertainty over the US economic recovery and geopolitics, the big carriers are unlikely to find much relief this year.

Task 3

(a) Case analysis (output text): STEP framework

Case study (input text): difficult year for business travellers

(b) She says she will focus on the big carriers because they are the ones who are suffering most.

(c) No: the case study is organised differently. It tells a story rather than giving a formal analysis. Organising the factors into STEP categories would not suit the structure of the story.

(d) No: for the same reason as (c).

(e) From her general understanding of what these concepts mean (the mind map in her mind). She read using these concepts to interpret the case study.

(f)   No, but it does use the following words in some sentences: *economic boom, economic recovery* and *geopolitic*. It also uses the words *economy fares* but this is a different meaning of the word *economy*.

(g)   From her general understanding of what these concepts mean (again, the mind map in her mind).

(h)   political <u>and</u> economic
        war with Iraq

      technological <u>and</u> economic
      use of the internet

      technological <u>and</u> social?
      use of the internet

(i)   No: the focus is on the organisation not the customers.

Activity 2.10

Task 1

Social: newspaper articles; downturn in passenger traffic; willingness to use low cost flights; willingness to use the internet.

Political: war with Iraq; government deregulation; threat of terrorism; cabin baggage regulations to enforce excess baggage fees; uncertain geopolitics; recession.

Technical: use of e-tickets to reduce costs; use of internet to obtain best fares.

Task 2

Economic: potential rise in oil prices; cut price or 'no frills' operators; impact of airlines filing for bankruptcy; uncertainty over health of economy; companies reconsidering business travel policies

Task 3

Cabin baggage regulations is possibly not an external factor influencing the airlines but a response by the airlines to the external factors. *Airlines filing for bankruptcy* may also not be an external factor.

Activity 2.11

(i) Government deregulation; (ii) potential rise in oil prices; (iii) use of e-tickets; (iv) use of internet to obtain best fares; (v) threat of terrorism; (vi) willingness to use low cost flights.

Activity 2.12

(a)   government deregulation – adapted
(b)   potential rise in oil prices – adapted
(c)   use of e-tickets – adapted
(d)   use of internet to obtain best fares – created
(e)   threat of terrorism – created

Activity 2.13

Nike trainers case study

Different spending power of consumers in different countries (E)

Fashion trends (S)

Popular culture (S)

Beneficial trade and tariff agreements (P)

Range of market sectors (S/E)

Unauthorised supermarket imports (E)

Age (S)

e-commerce (T)

Home Insulation case study

Reduction of grant aid (E)

Vodafone case study

American lead in internet exploitation (E/T)

Threat from US potential to move to third generation technology (T)

Convergence of communication devices (T)

High costs of government licences (P)

High cost of network spending and handset subsidies (E)

Mannesmann case study

Risk of takeover (E)

Tony Blair pressure on German company (P)

Suspicion of stock markets (S)

Activity 2.14

(a) A significant rise in oil prices <u>would further add</u> to the economic pressure on the industry.

(b) The **use of the internet by both business and leisure passengers** <u>has enabled</u> travelers to compare prices between airlines and select the most cost-effective route and itinerary.

(c) The terrorist attacks of September 11th 2001 and the threat of similar attacks in the future <u>have made</u> passengers more reluctant to travel.

(d) **the use of internet booking systems** has also <u>enabled airlines to reduce</u> their overheads.

Activity 2.17

Extract C, interest; extract D, power.

Activity 2.18

Task 2

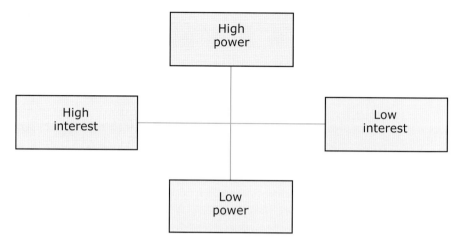

Figure 2.9   Answer to Activity 2.18, Task 2

Task 3

Figure 2.10   Answer to Activity 2.18, Task 3

Activity 2.19

The order of categories in the extract is A, C, B and D.

Activity 2.20

Paragraph 1

The AA and stakeholders with high power and high interest (category D)

The key players were the Director-General of the AA and   C
his immediate management team carrying out the
strategic review, as well as the full members of the AA.
John Maxwell and his management team were key
players with high power and high interest ...

as their planning and decision making would determine   R
their future with the AA, the future of the AA, the future
of those who worked for the AA, and the future of AA
members.

The full members would collectively decide whether the AA was to demutualise. They might have chosen to support any demutualisation recommendations made by John Maxwell and his team, or to reject them in favour of a bidder, such as Ford, buying the AA.   R

Paragraph 2

The AA and stakeholders with high power and low interest (category C)

The merchant bank Schroders was a category C stakeholder ...   C

as it had relatively little interest in whether the AA finally decided to demutualise. However, as corporate adviser to the AA, it was relatively powerful as it was able to advise and potentially influence John Maxwell and his management team.   R

Paragraph 3

The AA and stakeholders with low power and high interest (category B)

The category B stakeholders, those with high interest and low power in the demutualisation issue, included associate members and employees.   C

The associate members clearly had a high interest in whether or not the AA decided to demutualise. The primary concerns for associate members were the effect of demutualisation on the services they received and the cost of associate membership. However, as non-voting members, associates had no direct power to influence the outcome of any ballot on demutualisation.   R

Equally, employees had a high interest in the future of the AA and would be concerned as to the effects of demutualisation. Potential effects of demutualisation could have included the AA becoming more competitive and this being achieved via cost cutting and job losses. However, employees had no direct role in the ballot and would ultimately have to accept its outcome.   R

Paragraph 5

The AA and stakeholders with low power and low interest (category A)

The category A stakeholders are those with low power and low interest. For the AA, non-members fell into this category.   C

They were unable to receive breakdown services from the organisation and had no influence over its demutualisation decision.   R

SESSION 3 Recognising influences and impacts

© Mike Baldwin / Cornered

3.1 Introduction

Sessions 1 and 2 introduced mapping a case and using business concepts to analyse it. Session 2 introduced **factors** influencing businesses according to a STEP framework. In addition, you studied the relationship between a company and its **stakeholders**. You may recall that there were many events and actions in the cases you studied. In each case, these were related in some way. By understanding the relationship between events and actions you get a better insight into the organisation. This session will take you through the process of identifying an important feature of the relationship between events: which factors **influence** the organisation and what their **impacts** are. This relationship is similar to **cause-and-effect** relationships in everyday life: something **causes** something else to happen. The words **influence** and cause and **impact** and effect are used interchangeably in this session.

Almost all of your actions are caused by some other actions or events and situations. In the next activity you will reflect on these ideas.

Activity 3.1 ....

Purpose: to note the relationships between events and actions in everyday life.

Task: consider the two situations below. Which event or action is a cause? Which one is an effect? Which words could you use to combine the two sentences in each situation?

Situation 1

It snowed heavily. I did not go to work.

Situation 2

England lost the football match to Spain. My son cried.

Compare your answers with those suggested in the Answer section.

Comment ....

In both Situations 1 and 2 one event caused something to happen. One event is followed by another because of the first. This relationship can be shown in a diagram such as Figure 3.1.

| Heavy snow | ⟶ | Not going to work |

Cause   **Effect**

Figure 3.1 Cause-and-effect relationship in everyday life

There are two things to remember here: what is the relationship between the two events and which event happened first? There is a cause and effect relationship between the two events. The cause comes before the effect. This kind of relationship applies to the business world as well.

Learning outcomes

In this session, you will practise the following skills:

- identifying cause-and-effect relationships between events and actions in a business situation
- noting the different orders in which the cause and the effect are presented according to the writer's purpose
- understanding various types of cause-and-effect relationships
- using 'cause-and-effect' words and expressions
- analysing cause-and-effect relationships in a business case analysis.

It is important that you relate this session back to the activities you carried out and the concepts you learned in Sessions 1 and 2.

Activity 3.2 ....

Purpose: to become familiar with cause-and-effect relationships in a business situation.

Task: read extract A below which is about the relationship between people's earnings and the sales growth of a company. Then answer the following questions.

1   What is the factor influencing clothes retailers such as Marks & Spencer?

2   Use key words from the extract or make up your own (use noun groups as you practised in Sessions 1 and 2) to fill in the boxes in Figure 3.2. They show the relationship between events in the extract.

Extract A

If people earn more money, they will have extra money to spend on goods. This will have an impact on retail industries such as the clothes industry. Clothes retailers such as Marks & Spencer will be able to sell more of their products. This means that products are likely to become cheaper.

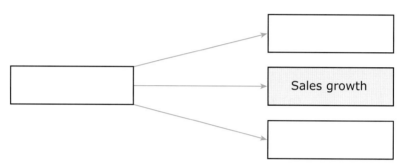

Figure 3.2   The cause-and-effect relationship in business

Compare your answers with those suggested in the Answer section.

Comment

This activity has given you an opportunity to see how one thing causes another or one thing happens because of another. A certain factor such as people's earnings influences the clothes retail market. This is an economic factor in the STEP framework like the ones you considered in Session 2. Note that the event which influences happens first, followed by its impact or effect. For example, people earn more money before they can spend more.

Generally, writers use a **signal word** to indicate a cause or an effect. In extract A, the word *if* is used in the first half of the first sentence. This indicates a cause (people's better earnings) which leads to an effect (having more money to spend). Other signal words in the extract are *impact* and *mean*. These words are useful 'cause-and-effect' signposts to the reader. You will meet many of them in this session.

3.2 Causes and effects in case studies

As already noted, almost all of your actions cause some kind of effect or they are the effects of some other actions in everyday life. The same applies to a company or a business. What a company decides to do is caused by some other events or actions and its decision is likely to bring about changes. For example, when there is a political crisis in the Middle East, petroleum retailers increase their oil prices. As a result, other retailers increase the price of their products.

Business cases are stories about **what** a company does, **how** it does what it does and **why** it does what it does. So, cause-and-effect relationships are inherently central to business cases. Being able to recognise this relationship gives you a better insight into the business world. It is often done by analysing business case study texts in business studies from a 'cause-and-effect' perspective. Therefore, it is essential to learn how to identify causes and effects. Next you will look at some case study assignment questions.

Activity 3.3 ···

Purpose: to identify the words signalling cause-and-effect relationships in case study assignment questions.

Task: read the questions below which are from assignments in a business studies course. Students are required to analyse the events and actions in a company. This means they need to look at cause-and-effect relationships. Underline the words which indicate such relationships.

(a) What factors influence consumer demand for Gap's products?

(b) What impact has the Asda-WalMart takeover had on the marketing approaches adopted by Asda?

(c) Why is Nike the biggest training-shoe company in the world?

(d) Discuss the extent to which a large corporation such as Nike might influence the economic health of a developing country.

(e) What were the environmental pressures affecting Pilkington?

Compare your answers with those suggested in the Answer section.

Comment ··

This activity focused on some case study assignment questions where students need to explore cause-and-effect relationships in case studies. There are signal words which indicate this to students. If you don't recognise these signal words, you won't be able to respond to the question appropriately.

3.3 Identifying the cause and the effect

At a simple level, the cause answers the question '**Why** does something happen?' and the effect answers the question '**What** happens as a result?' There are three kinds of cause-and-effect relationship: (1) a simple one where one thing causes another; (2) a causal chain where something leads to an effect which causes a second effect, and so on; and (3) multi-causality, where one effect may have several causes or one cause may have several effects.

Activity 3.4 ....

Purpose: to match the cause–effect figures with the examples.

Task: the three types of cause and effect described above are shown in Figure 3.3(a), (b), (c) and (d). Match the figures with the examples following them. Each short text illustrates one type of relationship.

Type 1

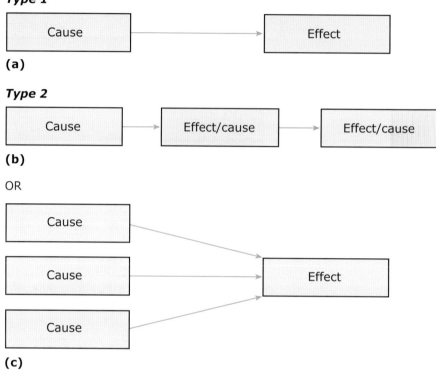

(a)

Type 2

(b)

OR

(c)

Type 3

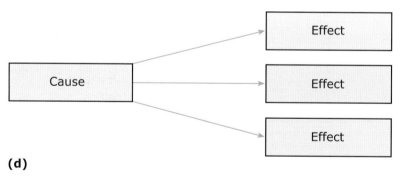

(d)

Figure 3.3   Different types of causal relationship

Texts

> 1   Sarah will be Acting Head of Section while Jane is on maternity leave. Clare and Alice will take over Sarah's post on a job-share basis during this period.
>
> 2   No one in the office was surprised to hear that Mina was appointed as Head of Sales. She is bright, has always worked hard and she got on with most people before her appointment.
>
> 3   Two new posts have been created as a result of expansion of the marketing section.

Compare your answers with those suggested in the Answer section.

The rest of the activities in this section explore these different types of cause–effect relationship. The text is about debt and credit. One of the features of the modern world is debt. People tend to buy goods for different reasons even when they don't have the money to pay for them. They use a facility called *credit*, which is provided by financial companies such as banks to pay for the goods (for example credit cards). Until they pay off the full amount they have borrowed, they are in debt. Many people in the UK face problems because they don't manage their personal finance well. They keep on using the credit facilities without making full payments. Banks and other financial organisations want to make sure that they don't lend money to someone who cannot make the payments. To ensure that they don't, these organisations work together with credit reference agencies (CRAs) which hold financial information about individuals. CRAs share the information with banks and other financial organisations. You may have heard of CRAs such as Experian and Equifax. The next case study deals with the external environment of CRAs in the face of current changes.

Activity 3.5   ....

Purpose: to comprehend the cause–effect relationships in a case study.

Task: read extract B below which is from the case study 'Debt in the UK and the role of credit reference agencies' and answer the questions in part A. Then answer the questions in part B.

Extract B

1   These days, **consumers** have become more comfortable with the idea of taking on debt. This seems to have applied to their attitudes to declaring **bankruptcy** as well when **levels of debt** become too high and they find that they are not able to make payments to their **creditors**. Such measures can mean that the individual is able to 'walk away' from their debts without having to pay them off. However, they may not be able to take on debt in the future.

2   As **personal insolvencies** hit another record high, new attitudes are driving the rise in the latest insolvency statistics. Rather than **suffer in debt** people are seeking a remedy to their debt anxieties. Bev Budsworth of The Debt Advisor says, 'Attitudes have changed towards debt fuelled by the unrealistic lifestyle aspirations from glossy magazines and TV makeover programmes. Twenty-five years ago, lifestyles were different and views towards money have subtly changed. Where **credit** was seen as debt, debt is now seen as credit, as a way of living the celebrity lifestyle.'

3   Figures released by the Department of Trade and Industry in February 2006 showed the number of personal insolvencies reached 20,461 in the fourth quarter of 2005 an increase of 15 per cent. The biggest rise was in **Individual Voluntary Arrangements** (IVA) with a 117 per cent increase in the last twelve months from 3206 to 6960.

4   Of course bankruptcy and IVAs are a two-sided coin. For every individual who has taken refuge from their creditors by using these facilities there is a **lender** who will see little or none of their **loan repaid**. Such

companies therefore use **credit reference agencies** to make sure that the people that they lend money to have a good **credit history** and will be more likely to pay the money back. What information do credit reference agencies use? Credit reference agencies hold information on most adults in the UK. This helps lenders to assess **the risk** of lending to particular people, and reduces the risk of **fraud**, by allowing them to look at information held in individual **credit files**.

Part A

Some of the key words in extract B are listed below. Choose the option that is nearest in meaning to the key words.

1   consumers
  (i)   people who buy and use goods or services
  (ii)   people or a company which make goods for others to use
  (iii) people who entertain others

2   bankruptcy
  (i)   a condition in which people borrow money from banks
  (ii)   a state of being unable to pay back the money borrowed from banks, individuals, etc.
  (iii) a situation where people have a huge amount of money to spend

3   levels of debt
  (i)   the amount of money a person lends someone
  (ii)   the amount of money a person deposits in a bank
  (iii) the amount of money a person borrows

4   creditor
  (i)   someone who borrows money from a person or company
  (ii)   someone or a company that lends money to a person
  (iii) someone who collects money for a company

5   personal insolvencies
  (i)   a state of a person being able to pay off their debts
  (ii)   a state of a person being unable to pay back the money borrowed
  (iii) a state of a person being able to solve their financial problems

6   suffer in debt
  (i)   suffer pain in silence
  (ii)   have no money to enjoy
  (iii) have financial pain

7   Individual Voluntary Arrangement (IVA)
  (i)   a formal agreement between a person and their creditor to pay off debts
  (ii)   an arrangement made by a person to volunteer
  (iii) an agreement by a volunteer

8   credit reference agencies
  (i)   companies that keep the information about a person's credit history
  (ii)   companies that keep records of a person's reference
  (iii) companies that hold records about people's personal lives

9 fraud
   (i)   a person is good at borrowing money
   (ii) a way of borrowing money
   (iii) a method of getting money from a person illegally
10 lender
   (i)   a company that distributes money
   (ii) a company that lets people borrow money for a charge
   (iii) a company that borrows money from other companies

Part B

Now that you studied the word groups above, next focus on the meaning in extract B. Answer the following questions.

1 Which factor causes people to declare bankruptcy?
2 What has affected people's attitudes towards debt?
3 Why do lenders seek information from credit reference agencies?

Compare your answers with those suggested in the Answer section.

Comment ....

You noted the key words used in extract B. You also looked at the relationship between them by answering the questions in Part B. These questions were essentially about the cause–effect relationship between **debt**, **credit**, **bankruptcy** and **credit reference agencies**.

Cause–effect relationships are complex. First, in a case study there may be many interrelated influences and impacts. Second, although the cause is always followed by the effect in the 'real' world, case writers present the cause followed by the effect, or the effect followed by the cause, depending on their topic and focus in the text. The next activity will help you explore this.

Activity 3.6   ....

Purpose: to extract the cause-and-effect events and sequence them.

Task: read extract B in Activity 3.5 again. Using two different coloured pens:

1   Underline the causes in one colour and the effects in another colour.

2   Write in the margin the order in which they are presented: C–E (cause followed by effect) or E–C (effect followed by cause).

3   Circle the words which signal the cause–effect relationship.

Compare your answers with those suggested in the Answer section.

Comment   ....

This activity shows three features of events in case studies.

1   They are not always presented in the order they may have happened. This is also quite normal in speaking. For example, you can say either 'I wore a coat because I was cold' or 'Because I was cold, I wore a coat'.

2   However, in speaking, the cause–effect relationship words are often quite simple: *because* is very common. In writing, as you have seen, there is a much wider range of words writers can use for cause–effect relationships. In the extract in Activity 3.5, for example, there is *can mean*, *fuelled*, *therefore*, *allowing* and *reduces*.

3   There are also cause–effect relationships with no signal words.

Recognising cause–effect relationship words is an important part of analysing business cases. In addition to what you saw in Activity 3.6, there are many other words which writers use to indicate cause–effect relationships in a case or its analysis. These are words which you could collect in a vocabulary notebook. The next activity introduces several such words in extracts from business studies course books.

Activity 3.7   ....

Purpose: to identify types of cause–effect relationship words.

Task: read the sentences below which describe causal relationships. There are four types of cause–effect words: verbs (e.g. *is driving*), **cause nouns** (e.g. *factor*), **effect nouns** (e.g. *impact*) and **causal linking words** (e.g. *due to*). Underline the cause–effect words in each sentence. Then write them in Table 3.1 in the category to which they belong.

Please note: these are **signal** words; you can still recognise a cause–effect relationship even if you don't know some of the other ideas in the sentences.

1   Very little of this periodic economic success appears to have been due to the operation of macro-economic policy.

2   The value of whatever money we may have in our pockets, or our bank accounts, shifts from moment to moment according to fluctuations in such markets. I would have no hesitation, therefore, in saying that globalisation, as we are experiencing it, is in many respects not only new, but revolutionary.

3　Political science has devoted relatively little attention to corporate governance which is regrettable since the company is the central institution of the market economy in Britain as elsewhere.

4　Because there is no tradition of state initiative to develop the economy, there is consequently little willingness by employers to accept levies to pay for training.

5　If the theory had been true, inflation should have been in double figures: instead it seemed low and stable.

6　These differences in the workings of markets are often a consequence of a variety of influences, such as historical forces and social, cultural and political factors.

7　This final section is about how societies can try to harness and govern markets so that they serve the needs of society rather than society having to serve every dictate of the market.

8　Social and political tensions, which have already risen sharply as a result of the recession, are further inflamed by large migratory movements to Western Europe.

9　Unless such conditions are present then the matrix can cause more problems than it solves.

10　It is hardly too much to say that the development of organisations was one of a number of major causes and inspirations behind the development not only of theories of organisation but of theories of modern society.

11　In general terms the culture of an organisation refers to those factors which enable us to distinguish one organisation from another and are the product of its history, management, operating environment, technology, goals, and so on.

12　Although this financial liberalisation helped to expand world commerce, it also produced another effect: the increasing separation of financial flows from trade in manufactures and services.

13　The influences of human relationships can most clearly be seen in the focus on managing the informal organisation.

14　In recent years new technologies have begun to influence organisational structures and to a large extent, open them up: the mobile phone, personal computers, lap-top computers, modems and networked databases.

15　This fits in with one of the key assumptions of our Business in Context model; that influences operate in more than one direction and while organizational factors such as structure can affect the outcome of a firm's activities, that outcome in turn affects the organization.

16　Ownership is important because of its potential impact on the way businesses are managed.

17　However they've managed to survive the last four years, they can't live without attending to the brute facts of corporate change and its effects on their own lives.

18　Consequently, we have been forced to make choices in considering which business processes to focus on.

19　Is globalisation a force promoting the general good?

Use Table 3.1 for categorisation. Some are already done to get you started.

Table 3.1 For use with Activity 3.7

No.	Cause verbs	Cause nouns	Effect nouns	Causal linking words
1				due to
2				
3				
4				
5				
6		influences	consequence	
7				
8	inflamed			
9				
10				
11				
12				
13				
14				
15				
16				
17				
18				
19				

Compare your answers with those suggested in the Answer section.

Comment

In difficult case studies, cause–effect signal words may show you where to focus in the case study but the relationships between events are not always signalled with cause–effect words. You may have to use your logic or interpretive skills to see the causal relationship and ask questions such as: 'Is there a relationship between these two events?'; 'If so, what is the relationship?'; 'Which is a cause and which is an effect?', and so on.

Activity 3.8

Purpose: to identify less obvious causal relationships in a situation.

Task: the use of the internet is having significant impacts on the business world. Many big retailers and shops use the internet to give information about their products and services to their potential customers. You may have tried some of them. Extract C below describes some of the impacts of the internet on business. Read it first to get an overview and then read it more carefully to answer the questions that follow it.

Extract C

Another factor fuelling the need for credit references has been the growth of e-commerce* where sales are projected to carry on growing robustly in the US, according to Forrester (an industry research body). Online retail sales will enjoy a 14% compound annual growth rate over the next five years. Excluding travel, sales will grow from nearly $110 billion this year to $210 billion in 2010. Also, in 2005, online sales reached a milestone when general merchandise sales topped $100 billion for the first time. The story is mirrored in the UK. During 2006, British retailers have made larger investments than ever before in their online services, in response to their customers' enthusiasm for them. The common availability of broadband has allowed retailers to present much higher quality product photographs and images – which are now often scaleable – and even explanatory videos. Real-time details of stock availability have become the norm. Delivery services are being transformed; for example, specific delivery time slots are becoming available for a growing number of non-food items, which is great news for people who are normally out during the day.

* e-commerce = use of electronic communications systems to buy and sell goods and services (for example, emails).

Part A

Which of the following statements are true?

1   In general, the impact of the growth of e-commerce has been positive.
2   Online sales are unlikely to grow in the next few years.
3   The retailers can give real-time information about their products and services.
4   The growth of e-commerce means a further need for credit references.

Part B

1   What is the effect(s) of the growth of e-commerce?
2   What evidence do you have to support your answer to question 1?

Compare your answers with those suggested in the Answer section.

Comment

In this task, you read a whole paragraph to find the effects of the growth of e-commerce. You had to make sense of the extract by dividing the events and the actions into groups and studying their relationship: whether one event or action led to the other. The high-level generalisation in the first sentence makes it clear that this paragraph is generally about a factor fuelling the need for credit references – the growth of e-commerce. After that, there are very few signals in the text to indicate causal relationships.

3.4 Cause–effect relationships and business models and concepts

Analysing a business case means using business concepts and models to understand the underlying issues in the case. Often this means understanding the cause–effect relationships in the case. In this section, you will focus on the cause–effect relationships underlying the STEP and the stakeholder frameworks.

The STEP framework

You will use the STEP framework to study a case called 'Debt in the UK and the role of credit reference agencies'. You have already studied paragraphs 8, 9 and 11 from this case in Activities 3.5 to 3.7. The case study describes people's changing attitudes towards debts. If you use a STEP framework to frame that event, you see that it is a sociological factor which has influenced the credit industry. You will use the STEP framework to identify other factors influencing the industry.

The case study is quite complicated. There are many events and, as you have seen, it may be difficult to tell which events really are influences. For this reason, when you do a STEP analysis it may be necessary to read through a case at least four times to:

1   get an overview
2   map the case
3   identify STEP factors
4   check that the factors you identify really do influence the organisation.

Activity 3.9

Purpose: to identify the factors responsible for changes in the credit industry.

Task: read Text 3.1 in Resource Book 1 and then work through the following steps.

1   First, map the case. Use some of the reading strategies introduced in Session 1 to produce brief notes or a mind map. Remember, these don't have to be very detailed. You need only a general overview.

2   Read the case again, looking for cause–effect signal words and circle them (there are more than 20).

3   Underline the factors which influence the credit reference industry. Use the cause–effect signal words to help you find them. But remember that not all factors will have cause–effect signals. Sometimes you have to interpret the influence.

4   Draw a STEP analysis table like the one below. Make key concept notes for the factors influencing the credit reference industry. (Use the methods introduced in Sessions 1 and 2.) Note: there won't be factors for all the categories. One example is already done for you.

STEP category	Factor
Sociological	Pressure on people to consume
Technological	
Economic	
Political	

Compare your answers with those suggested in the Answer section.

Comment   ....

This is quite a difficult task as factors overlap and one factor causes another. For example, consumers' willingness to use online services (a sociological factor) is caused by new developments in e-commerce (a technological factor). Therefore, it may not be clear whether an event is an environmental factor influencing the credit industry or the credit industry influencing the environment. It may sometimes be necessary to read through the case again, to check what impact each factor has.

Activity 3.10   ....

Purpose: to identify the impacts in a case study according to the STEP framework.

Task: in your STEP analysis table, number the factors you identified in Activity 3.9. Read Text 3.1 again, focusing on the impacts of the factors you identified. Write the impacts as key concepts and number them with their factor number. The impacts may not necessarily relate to the same factor. An example is given below.

STEP categories	Effects
Sociological	1 People's need to borrow money
Technological	
Economic	
Political	

Compare your answers with those suggested in the Answer section.

Comment   ....

This activity shows that most of the factors you listed in Activity 3.9 have a general impact on the CRA industry. The social factors create an environment in which debt and bankruptcy are acceptable. The technological factors make spending and getting credit easier. They also have a direct impact on the ways in which CRAs do business. You may have noted that, although there are more than 20 cause–effect signal words, there are not more than 20 factors which have a direct impact on the CRAs. This is because several of the cause–effect relationships are repeated and some of them don't directly impact on the companies but impact on other parts of the environment. However, all of the factors in Activity 3.9 can be seen as having a direct or an indirect impact on the CRAs.

The STEP framework in an output text

Using techniques similar to those you practised in the last two activities and in Sessions 1 and 2, a student produced a STEP analysis of the "Debt in the UK" text. The next few activities involve reading the first three paragraphs of this analysis to see how the cause–effect relationships were managed.

Purpose: to study the cause-and-effect language in a STEP analysis of the credit industry.

Task: you will need two different coloured pens for this activity. Read quickly through the STEP analysis below in extract D. Then using different coloured pens:

1   Underline all the factors in the analysis.

2   Underline all the impacts or effects.

3   Circle any words that are used to link the factor with its impact or the impact with the factor. One example is already done for you.

Extract D

Carry out a STEP analysis outlining the main factors in the external environment influencing the credit industry as presented in the 'Debt in the UK' case study.

This is a STEP analysis of the social, technological, economic and political factors that impact on the UK credit industry. The focus is on credit reference agencies (CRAs) which provide services to individuals and businesses.

The sociological factors identified in the case are as follows. Individuals' attitudes to debt are an important factor. They vary by consumer segments within the UK and also between countries. The case also points out that attitudes towards bankruptcy are changing – this means that the credit situation for retailers and others selling to the public is becoming riskier. In turn, this means a greater reliance by companies on the services offered by credit reference agencies (CRAs). Another factor fuelling the demand for credit references has been the rise in the use of credit cards. Use of credit cards has in turn been influenced by the rise in e-commerce – which people are increasingly willing to use, despite some of the risks associated with it. Below, the rise in e-commerce is seen as a technological development that has affected CRAs, but it should also be noted that consumers' willingness to use it reflects an attitudinal or social change.

Overall, technological factors affect the industry in two main ways. First, they can encourage spending and thereby the demand for credit, which will require the services of CRAs. Second, the way in which credit companies gather information about individuals will be affected by changes in technology. The case starts with a reference to the ease with which people can spend money and this is due to such aspects of technology as the internet and the telephone. The latter part of the case discusses the growth of e-commerce both now and in the future. Since payments for purchases on the internet are commonly paid using credit cards, the demand for credit references may rise as internet shopping increases. The case says that new developments in the way in which stores offer credit on the internet could also lead to a rise in levels of expenditure and the levels of debt. Another impact of new technology has been that the tools used by CRAs to assess the creditworthiness of individuals have also evolved.

Compare your answers with those suggested in the Answer section.

Comment ....

Cause–effect signal words and clauses

As you have seen, there is a wide range of cause–effect signal words. They help a reader understand the relationships between the events in a case study. In Activity 3.7 you identified four categories of them. The fourth category is **causal linking words**. These words link two or more ideas in a causal relationship. They may link two separate sentences, like this:

1   In September the company's share price continued to fall and it was obliged to dismantle two of its partnerships. **As a result**, Enron had to deduct $1 billion from its earnings for the third quarter of 2001.

Alternatively, they may link two parts of the same sentence, like this:

2   The collapse shocked the business world *since* Enron had been hailed as a highly successful company.

3   *Because* Wal-Mart has opened relatively few Wal-Mart superstores, the impact of the takeover has not been immediately felt by consumers.

The linking words in sentences 2 and 3 link two units of language inside one sentence. These units of language are called clauses.

Clauses are parts of sentences. Many clauses are just like sentences. They have a verb and a subject. For example, this is one sentence with two clauses:

The collapse shocked the business world

subject   verb

since

Enron had been hailed as a highly successful company.

subject   verb

Both clauses could be sentences on their own. However, when they are linked with the word *since*, they become two parts of the same sentence. The two parts are both clauses.

When the parts of a sentence are linked together with obvious causal linking words: *since*, *because*, *as* or *so*, it is quite easy to see which is the cause and which is the effect.

However, cause-and-effect clauses can be linked in less obvious ways. The first sentence in (1) above also has two clauses. They are joined by the linking word *and*. This is not an obvious causal linking word but the two clauses are actually a cause and an effect.

In September the company's share price continued to fall   [cause]

subject   verb

and

it   was obliged to dismantle two of its partnerships.   [effect]

subject   verb

The next activity looks at how the cause-and effect-clauses are linked in several sentences.

Activity 3.12 ....

Purpose: to identify the linking words which show the cause-and-effect relationship.

Task: carefully read extract E below. Circle the words that link the cause–effect clauses in each sentence. Underline the cause in one colour and the effect in another colour.

> *Extract E*
>
> 1   Workers at the mine in northern Chile began the walkout yesterday morning after management failed to meet demands to boost wages almost 17 per cent, said Pedro Marin, a spokesman for the union. (Source: *The Toronto Star*, 2006.)
>
> 2   Other airlines have begun to charge an additional fee of up to $25 if passengers insist on using paper tickets instead of electronic ones. Until they reversed themselves a few weeks ago, many of the big airlines had also begun to charge passengers $100 if they wanted to fly standby on flights on the same day as their originally scheduled flights. (Source: 'US Airlines' case study.)
>
> 3   The shine was first tarnished in 1992, when an American reporter stumbled upon a factory in Saipan, in the Pacific, where Gap clothes were being produced by a subcontractor who, unknown to Gap, was hiring Chinese labourers for 80-hour weeks at less than $2 an hour. (Source: 'Gap' case study.)
>
> 4   Analysts knew things were bad when, during the busy back-to-school period, the company was offering 20% discounts. Gap seldom promotes cut-price offers. The company moved quickly to clear up the inventory problems which had led to late deliveries and began a new television advertising campaign in November 2000. (Source: 'Gap' case study.)
>
> 5   However, senior managers have a legal responsibility to the shareholders and will be heavily influenced by shareholder interest. Gap's poor performance in 2001, for example, prompted the company to make over a thousand staff redundant, demonstrating that shareholders are more powerful stakeholders than employees. When performance is poor, management is accountable to shareholders, not employees and will make such decisions accordingly. (Source: 'Gap' case study.)

Compare your answers with those suggested in the Answer section.

Comment ....

This activity focused on some less obvious linking words which show the cause–effect relationship between clauses. You may also have noted that there were other causes and effects in these sentences. Not all cause–effects are clauses linked by causal linking words. As you have seen in this session, there are many ways in which cause–effect can be shown in a case study. Looking for obvious cause–effect linking words can be useful in finding these. However, there will probably be other causes and effects which are less obvious – either because the link words are not obvious or because the cause–effect is signalled by another kind of word (such as the nouns and verbs you identified in Activity 3.7) or because there is no signal word and you have to interpret whether the events described have a cause-and-effect relationship.

The stakeholder model and cause and effect

Like the STEP framework, the stakeholder model is also used to study the external environment of a business. The stakeholders of a company include those people and organisations who are directly or indirectly interested in the company's success. The factors in the STEP framework are somehow related to what the stakeholders of a company do. For example, the willingness of the customers (one of the stakeholders) and their ability to use the internet (sociological and technological factors) influences the way businesses sell their products and CRAs offer their services.

While analysing a business case using the stakeholder model, you need to identify who the stakeholders are and how they influence the organisation, based on their power and interest in it.

If the *power* of a stakeholder is high, their influence on the organisation is high. If the *interest* of a stakeholder is high, the impacts of the organisation's actions on them will be high. This means there is always a cause-and-effect relationship between what happens in the company or what it decides to do and its stakeholders' reactions as the next activity shows.

Activity 3.13 ....

Purpose: to identify an organisation's stakeholders and their relationship with it.

Task: this activity involves a case study text about Gap, an international clothes retailer. Recently, it has faced problems with sales growth and working conditions. In response, some stakeholders have acted. Also in response, the company too has acted. Read Text 3.2 in Resource Book 1 to the end of the section 'Sourcing of manufactured goods', to get an overview of the situation. Use the reading strategies you have learned in Sessions 1 and 2. Then answer the following questions.

1   Who are the main stakeholders of Gap?

2   Why have Africa Forum and Unite campaigned against Gap? Which factor was responsible for this?

Compare your answers with those suggested in the Answer section.

Comment ....

This activity was built on what you studied in Session 2 in terms of categorising stakeholders. Basically, stakeholder analysis is a cause–effect analysis. The company sees that a company action will cause a stakeholder reaction. There are then two questions for the company: (1) 'How much does the stakeholder care about this cause–effect situation?' and (2) 'How much does the company care about the cause–effect situation?' The answer to the first question relates to the stakeholder's interest. The answer to the second question relates to the stakeholder's power. These questions are important because there is likely to be conflict between stake-holders. For example, shareholders are generally interested in profits while employees are interested in better salaries and benefits. However, shareholders may be more powerful than employees.

Clearly, there are cause–effect relationships in these actions and events initiated by either the company or its stakeholders.

Activity 3.14   ....

Purpose: to identify the actors, actions, causes and effects in a stakeholder analysis.

Task: Table 3.2 gives information about the main actors, their actions, and the causes and effects of these actions in Text 3.2, which you read in the previous activity. There is information missing from the numbered empty boxes in the table. Write in the missing information from the case study. Use your note-making skills for this task.

Table 3.2   For use with Activity 3.14

Actor	Action	Cause	Effects
The company	change chief executive	1	
	support and benefits to staff		
	2		ranked 2 for support of women employees
	outsourcing to vendors	3	
	4	criticisms of sweat shops newspaper article	
	sacked contractor	5	
	6	serious breach of code of conduct	

Senior management	7		decline in sales	unsuccessful
8	employment of workers at very low wages for 80 hours a week in 1992		To make economic profits	9
Vendor compliance officers	monitoring and evaluation of Gap-approved garment producers		10	
	11		as above	
	acting as an advocate for vendors' employees		as above	
Development campaigners	public criticism		12	negative impact on Gap's sales
	call for consumer boycott		as above	as above
Consumers	13		exploitation in developing countries by Gap's suppliers	decline in Gap's sales

Compare your answers with those suggested in the Answer section.

Comment

Many of the actions of the company and the stakeholders are caused by other actions or situations. The company actions impact on the stakeholders and the stakeholders' actions impact on the company. First, you should decide what the cause–effect relationships are. Then you can decide what to do, based on the power and interests of the stakeholders involved.

3.5 The cause–effect language of case studies

Case studies are stories of how one event leads to another. It is the cause-effect language which holds the stories together and explains why one event leads to another.

Activity 3.15 ....

Purpose: to use the words and expressions associated with cause and effect.

Task: carefully read extract F below, which is from the 'Minding the Gap' text. Words or expressions with cause-and-effect meanings are deleted and given alongside each paragraph. Fill in the spaces by choosing from among them correctly. Remember to use the correct *form* of the word to fit in the sentence.

Extract F

Text	Cause-and-effect meanings
After a 16 year period of sustained growth, Gap experienced a serious decline in sales and profits during 2000. [...] Initially it was felt that this was ... the broader economic slowdown in the US, in turn ... a slump in the stock market and rises in interest rates ... long-standing high levels of debt amongst American consumers. This was thought to ... sales in the clothing retail sector particularly sharply. In one assessment of the state of the sector, Wendy Liebmann, president of WSL Strategic Retail, a firm of market analysts, said: 'A combination of the economy and the elections ... consumers nervous. That sort of nervousness ... the retail sector across the board, but it ... apparel first.'	affect make combine with due to hit hit spark by
While The Gap was not the only clothing company to have ... the downturn in consumer confidence, others seemed relatively ... Low-cost operators such as Wal-Mart, a direct competitor to Old Navy, were continuing to do well. For Gap however, the changing economic conditions merely ... internal problems of 'uninspiring merchandise and poor management.'	highlight suffer from unscathed
After initially ... a combination of the economic slowdown and bad weather earlier in the year, by September executives were ... 'inventory problems, heavy markdowns and a ... advertising campaign which focused on in-store promotions rather than brand-building slots on television.' Analysts knew things were bad ... during the busy back-to-school period, the company was offering 20% discounts. Gap seldom promotes cut-price offers. The company moved quickly to clear up the inventory problems which had ... late deliveries and began a new television advertising campaign in November 2000. It also recruited new heads of marketing for Banana Republic and Old Navy.	admit to blame dispiriting however lead to when

Compare your answers with those suggested in the Answer section.

Comment

This activity focused on both the obvious and the ambiguous cause-and-effect words. Words such as 'when' can be ambiguous as in extract F. It may mean time or it may introduce a cause. In this particular context, both seem to be possible. It could mean Gap's situation became bad because it was offering 20 per cent discount, as reinforced by the following sentence in the text ('Gap seldom promotes cut-price offers') or simply that was the time when things were bad. The other words are mostly verbs. Also some words, although not necessarily a cause or effect word, indicate a cause–effect relationship because of the specific context the expression is used in (for example, blaming a combination).

There is such a wide range of words and expressions having cause-and-effect meanings, you are advised to keep a record of them when you meet them during the course. (See the vocabulary-building activity at the end of this session.)

Activity 3.16

Purpose: to examine a stakeholder analysis of a company.

Task: next you will read a stakeholder analysis of the Gap case study written by a student on a business studies course. This output text was a high-scoring analysis in response to this assignment task:

Use the stakeholder model of business environments to critically examine the external environment of Gap Inc. outlined in the case study.

Read Text 3.3 in Resource Book 1 and answer the following questions.

1   How is the analysis organised (i.e. introduction, topics, categories, etc.)?
2   Which two concepts frame the analysis?
3   Which stakeholders are given priority in the organisation? Why?
4   Underline in one colour the words and expressions associated with 'power' or 'influence'.
5   In a different colour, underline the words and expressions associated with 'interest'.
6   In a different colour, underline the words and expressions signalling cause–effect.
7   What, in your view, is the relationship between power, interest and cause–effect?

Compare your answers with those suggested in the Answer section.

Comment

This activity presented a sample stakeholder analysis done by a student such as you. The key concepts (power and interest) are used to control the analysis and the organisation of the output text. They frame the analysis. Cause-and-effect language is used to explain why particular stakeholders belong in a particular category and to describe how they respond to particular events and situations. There are some obvious words signalling power, interest and cause–effect; there are also less obvious words which you have to use if you are doing a stakeholder analysis.

3.6 Vocabulary activity

See the course website for how to do a vocabulary-building activity for this session.

3.7 Application activities

Activity 3.17

Purpose: to use the skills learned in this session to write up a stakeholder analysis of an organisation.

Task: read Text 3.4 in Resource Book 1, using active reading strategies to map the case. Then make notes to frame the case using a stakeholder analysis. Decide whether you will frame the stakeholders using the framework from either the AA analysis or the Nike and Gap analyses. Write up a stakeholder analysis of the copper mining companies in Escondida. Remember to use *power* and *interest* to frame your analysis. When you have finished, there is an example of a written-up analysis in Resource Book 1 to compare yours with (Text 3.5).

Check your answer with the one suggested in the Answer section.

3.8 Critical reflection

Think about the following questions.

1   Does knowledge of cause-and-effect relationships help you to understand the business world?

2   Does knowledge of the language of cause–effect relationships help you to understand the business world?

3.9 Review

After studying this session, you should have developed your skills in:

- identifying cause-and-effect relationships between or among events and actions inside and outside an organisation
- understanding the value of cause-and-effect relationships in a case study analysis
- identifying the words and expressions with cause-and-effect meanings and using them effectively
- noting the organisation of a case study analysis
- writing up a case study analysis using a business framework.

3.10 Answer section

Activity 3.1

Situation 1

The first event is a cause and the second event is an effect.

You could use *because*, *since* or *as* to combine the two sentences:

As/ Because / Since it snowed heavily, I did not go to work.

Situation 2

The first event is a cause and the action in the second sentence is an effect. The two sentences can be combined using *because*, *since* or *as*:

My son cried *because/ since/ as* England lost the football match to Spain.

Activity 3.2

People's earnings
See Figure 3.4.

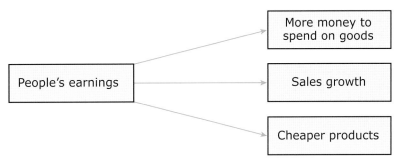

Figure 3.4   Answer to Activity 3.2

Activity 3.3

(a) What <u>factors</u> <u>influence</u> consumer demand for Gap's products?
(b) What <u>impact</u> has the Asda–Wal-Mart takeover had on the marketing approaches adopted by Asda?
(c) <u>Why</u> is Nike the biggest training-shoe company in the world?
(d) Discuss the extent to which a large corporation such as Nike might <u>influence</u> the economic health of a developing country.
(e) What were the environmental <u>pressures</u> <u>affecting</u> Pilkington?

Activity 3.4

Text 1 = type 2; text 2 = type 3 (first figure); text 3 = type 1.

Activity 3.5

Part A
1 (i); 2 (ii); 3 (iii); 4 (ii); 5 (ii); 6 (iii); 7 (i); 8 (i); 9 (iii); 10 (ii).

Part B

1   There are two factors causing bankruptcy for people: high levels of debt and being unable to pay off debts.

2   People's attitudes towards debt have changed because they view debt as credit and they have a desire to live a celebrity life inspired by glossy magazines and television programmes.

3   Lenders seek information from credit reference agencies because they hold the information about an individual's credit history and lenders want to make sure that they lend the money to someone who can pay off the debt in time.

Activity 3.6

The causes are underlined and the effects are in bold type. Some parts are both underlined and bold because they represent both the cause and the effect. The words signalling the cause–effect relationship are in square brackets.

when levels of debt become too high [and] **they find that they are not able to make payments to their creditors**.	C–E
Such measures [can mean] **that the individual is able to 'walk away' from their debts without having to pay them off**, however, **they may not be able to take on debt in the future**.	C–E C–E
As personal insolvencies hit another record high, new attitudes [are driving] **the rise in the latest insolvency statistics**.	C–E
Bev Budsworth of The Debt Advisor says, "**Attitudes have changed towards debt** [fuelled by]the unrealistic lifestyle aspirations from glossy magazines and TV makeover programmes.	E–C
Of course bankruptcy and IVAs are a two-sided coin. [For] every individual who has taken refuge from their creditors by using these facilities **there is a lender who will see little or none of their loan repaid. Such companies** [therefore] **use credit reference agencies to make sure that the people that they lend money to have a good credit history and will be more likely to pay the money back**.	C– E– E
What information do credit reference agencies use? Credit reference agencies hold information on most adults in the UK. This **[helps] lenders to assess the risk of lending to particular people**, and **[reduces] the risk of fraud**, [by allowing] them to look at information held in individual credit files.	C– E E–C

Activity 3.7

No.	Cause verbs	Cause nouns	Effect nouns	Causal linking words
1				due to
2				according to therefore
3				since
4				because consequently
5				if
6		influences forces factors	consequence	
7				so that
8	are inflamed			as a result of
9	cause			unless … then
10		causes inspirations		
11		factors	product	
12	Helped to expand produced		effect	
13		influences		
14	influence			
15	affect affects	influences factors		
16			impact	because of
17			effects	
18	have been forced			consequently
19	promoting	force		

Activity 3.8

Part A
The true statements are: 1, 3 and 4.

Part B
1   The effects of e-commerce are:
    (i)   demand for credit references
    (ii)   online retail sales growth
    (iii) more investments in the retail industry in the UK
    (iv)   the possibility for customers to see higher quality product photographs, images and explanatory videos which give better information about products
    (v)   real-time information about stock availability
    (vi)   better delivery service
    (vii) convenient for customers.

2   There are some clues which indicate causal links in the text. Some of them are obvious while others are not.

(i)   Demand for credit references – *another factor fuelling*

(ii)   Online retail sales growth – no obvious clues given except your own interpretation. There is a verb – *enjoy* – which may suggest a positive impact and the statistics also show the growth.

(iii) More investments in the retail industry in the UK – *in response to their customers' enthusiasm for them* (online services).

(iv)   The possibility for customers to see higher quality product photographs, images and explanatory videos which give better information about products – there is no direct clue but the verb *allowed* indicates the effect of broadband which is part of e-commerce.

(v)   Real-time information about stock availability – no obvious clue but this can be linked with the common availability of broadband.

(vi)   Better delivery service – no obvious clue but it is associated with developments in e-commerce.

(vii) Convenient for customers – as in (vi).

Activity 3.9

2

[P1] this pressure, means; [P2] may mean, because; [P3] all change with, if, impact, boosted; [P4] depend; [P5] responses; [P6] has helped to, may well cause; [P7] impact; [P8] can mean; [P9] are driving, fuelled by; [P10] mean; [P11] factor fuelling, in response to, has allowed, are being transformed; has meant that, has to evolve with.

4

STEP category	Factor
Sociological	1 Pressure on people to consume or need to borrow money 2 Change of individuals' attitudes towards debt 3 Publicity about private debt levels 4 People's willingness to declare bankruptcy 5 Greater tendency of people to use credit cards 6 Consumers' willingness to use online services
Technological	7 Availability of online credit service (Bill Me Later) to consumers 8 Huge growth in e-commerce 9 Broadband or better advertising of products 10 The internet and telephone shopping 11 New online tools for credit assessment

Activity 3.10

STEP factors	Effects
Sociological	People's willingness to take on more debt (sociological factors 1, 2, 4) Change in people's spending habit (sociological factors 1, 2, 4, 5 & 6 and technological factors 7, 8 and 10))
Technological	Sales growth in e-commerce (technological factors 7 and 8 and sociological factors 5 and 6) Convenient ways of spending money (technological factors 8 and 10) Evolving method of credit assessment by CRAs (technological factor 11)

Activity 3.11

The factors are in **bold** type; the impacts are underlined; and the cause–effect words are boxed .

Carry out a STEP analysis outlining the main factors in the external environment influencing the credit industry as presented in the 'Debt in the UK' case study

This is a STEP analysis of the social, technological, economic and political factors that impact on the UK credit industry. The focus is on credit reference agencies (CRAs) which provide services to individuals and businesses.

The sociological factors identified in the case are as follows. **Individuals' attitudes to debt** are an important factor. They vary by consumer segments within the UK and also between countries. The case also points out that **attitudes towards bankruptcy** are changing – this means that the credit situation for retailers and others selling to the public is becoming riskier. In turn, **this** means a greater reliance by companies on the services offered by credit reference agencies (CRAs). Another factor fuelling the demand for credit references has been **the rise in the use of credit cards**. Use of credit cards has in turn been influenced by **the rise in e-commerce** – which people are increasingly willing to use, despite some of the risks associated with it. Below, **the rise in e-commerce** is seen as a technological development that has affected CRAs, but it should also be noted that **consumers' willingness to use it** reflects an attitudinal or social change.

Overall, technological factors affect the industry in two main ways. Firstly, **they** can encourage spending and thereby the demand for credit, which will require the services of CRAs. Second, the way in which credit companies gather information about individuals will be affected by **changes in technology**. The case starts with a reference to the ease with which people can spend money and this is due to **such aspects of technology as the internet and the telephone**. The latter part of the case discusses the growth of e-commerce both now and in the future. Since **payments for purchases on the internet are commonly paid using credit cards**, the demand for credit references may rise as **internet shopping increases**. The case says that new developments in **the way in which stores offer credit on the internet** could also lead to a rise in levels of expenditure and the levels of debt. Another impact of **new technology** has been that the tools used by CRAs to assess the creditworthiness of individuals have also evolved.

Activity 3.12

Effects are <u>underlined</u>; causes are boxed; causal link words are in **bold**.

1   <u>Workers at the mine in northern Chile began the walkout yesterday morning</u> **after** management failed to meet demands to boost wages almost 17 per cent, said Pedro Marin, a spokesman for the union.

2   <u>Other airlines have begun to charge an additional fee of up to $25</u> **if** passengers insist on using paper tickets instead of electronic ones . Until they reversed themselves a few weeks ago, <u>many of the big airlines had also begun to charge passengers $100</u> **if** they wanted to fly standby on flights on the same day as their originally scheduled flights.

3   <u>The shine was first tarnished in 1992,</u> **when** an American reporter stumbled upon a factory in Saipan, in the Pacific , where Gap clothes were being produced by a subcontractor who, unknown to Gap, was hiring Chinese labourers for 80-hour weeks at less than $2 an hour.

4   <u>Analysts knew things were bad</u> **when,** during the busy back-to-school period, the company was offering 20% discounts . Gap seldom promotes cut-price offers. The company moved quickly to clear up the inventory problems which had led to late deliveries and began a new television advertising campaign in November 2000.

5   However, senior managers have a legal responsibility to the shareholders **and** <u>will be heavily influenced by shareholder interest.</u> Gap's poor performance in 2001, for example, prompted the company to make over a thousand staff redundant, demonstrating that shareholders are more powerful stakeholders than employees. **When** performance is poor , <u>management are accountable to shareholders, not employees and will make such decisions accordingly.</u>

Activity 3.13

1   The main stakeholders of Gap are the shareholders (the Fisher family and others), the senior management, other employees, customers, vendors, special interest groups or not-for-profit organisations and the media.

2   The main reason for Africa Forum and Unite to campaign against Gap is 'abusive working conditions' in Gap's vendors' factories in at least six countries. The external factors responsible for their actions are economic (low pay), political or legal (long hours of work which is against the law) and sociological (health hazards?).

Activity 3.14

The missing information is:

1   retirement of Drexler and sales decline

2   diversity or equal opportunities action

3   gives greater flexibility

4   control of vendors by code of conduct

5　newspaper article

6　terminate business with vendors

7　attempt to stop decline in sales

8　vendors

9　termination of Gap's business

10　abusive working conditions

11　enforcing corrective action on health and safety;

12　long hours, low pay, health hazards, exploitative management

13　not spending as much on Gap products as they used to.

Activity 3.15

The words in order are: due to, sparked by, combined with, affect, are making, hits, hits, suffered from, unscathed, highlighted, blaming, admitting to, dispiriting, when, led to.

Activity 3.16

1　The analysis is clearly divided into different sections of sub-topics: 'Introduction', 'Gap stakeholders', 'How much influence does each stakeholder possess' and 'Conclusion'. First the main stakeholders are identified. Next, how each of the principal stakeholders influences the company is discussed. The most dominant stakeholders (shareholders and the management) and their influence are presented first followed by less powerful stakeholders.

2　The two key concepts are *power* or *influence* and *interest* of stakeholders. These concepts run throughout the analysis.

3　The shareholders (and the management) are given priority in the company because they 'own' the company and they are the investors. The management are accountable to them. The shareholders are the most powerful stakeholders although they may be influenced by the external factors such as economy and technology. The company exists because of the stakeholders even if consumers decide whether to keep the company or not. On the other hand, the workers and their union also appear to be very powerful stakeholders as there is a huge impact on the company because of their actions (campaign).

4　The 'power' or 'influence' words are: *influence, power groups, influence, make over a thousand staff redundant, are accountable to shareholders, will make such decisions, chose not to, he could have had he so wished, powerful, own, exert little influence, it can simply, it is Gap's requirement that ... not vice versa, to ensure, have a good deal of influence, can influence, on the periphery of Gap's external environment, use the media to highlight their agenda, influence, relatively powerful, are the most powerful stakeholder, have the power to determine, has little say in the company decision making, compete for influence, dominant stakeholders, was accountable to them, are the weakest players, holds the upper hand, hold the key to, use their power, enlightened.*

5   The interest words are: *stakeholders* (many examples), *have an interest, special interest groups.*

6   The cause–effect words are: *this is not surprising after all, for this reason, if, based on a number of factors, other factors serve to, prompt, because, ensures that, unless.*

7   Cause–effect language explains why powerful stakeholders are powerful and why they act in the way they do; it describes how they act and how different groups impact on each other. Cause–effect language relates to stakeholder interest by describing how people or groups are affected by the company's actions or by other groups.

Activity 3.17

Escondida stakeholder analysis

The case presents the situation at a copper mine in Chile. The mine appears to be a joint venture between two western companies, BHP Billiton and Rio Tinto and Codelco, the Chilean state-mining company. The key issue addressed by the case is the strike being mounted by workers for better pay in the face of rising prices for the mine's output, which is copper. Chile is one of the world's major producers of copper and reference is also made in the case to China, which is one of the largest consumers.

High interest and high power stakeholders

These are the stakeholders who have a high level of interest in the strike and a high level of power in being able to influence the outcome.

In this category I could place the following groups. The 'Escondida's workers' union Number 1' derives its power from the fact that it represents the workers and would also have a high level of interest in resolving the situation. However, the level of power that it enjoys seems to be disputed by BHP Billiton who claim that, rather than representing 94% of workers, it actually represents 70%.

The other party in the negotiation is the employers and they would be represented by the mine owners who are BHP Billiton and Codelco. These organisations would also have a high level of interest in seeing the dispute resolved. In BHP Billiton's case, this would be because the mine represents a significant proportion of its total profits. In the case of Codelco, the interest would be because of the possible impact on the rest of the Chilean mining industry. Also, having a high level of interest but perhaps less power would be Rio Tinto which has a share in the mine (which is slightly more than half of BHP Billiton's).

Note that the actual level of power enjoyed by Rio Tinto depends on the nature of the agreements entered into by the three joint venture partners. Indeed, while they may have a high level of interest in the outcome, the level of power enjoyed by the actual management of the mine will depend on the level of central control exerted by the three mine owners.

Low power and high interest

In terms of stakeholders with low power and a high level of interest, the group in this category would be individual workers – because on their own these people would have very little ability to exert any influence on the organisation. Their power is derived by being able to negotiate on a collective basis.

Low power and low interest

The case refers to contractors being used to run the equipment. They may have an interest in the outcome in so far as it influences their work, but there seems to be no explicit cause for their being able to exercise any power.

The case mentions that China is the world's largest buyer of copper and you can only assume that it may have an interest and power in the outcome, because there is no reference to any power being exercised. High interest can be inferred because of the country's position as a copper consumer. Similarly, although only passing reference is made to Chile as a country, you could assume that the government of the country has a high level of interest in the outcome but the level of power it can exert will depend on its relationship with Codelco (the state copper producer).

SESSION 4 Identifying problems

A train wreckage at Montparnasse station, Paris, 1895

4.1 Introduction

You have now practised three of the skills involved in doing a case study analysis. These are mapping the case, framing the case, and noting influences and impacts. This session focuses on the fourth skill in this process – identifying problems.

From your reading and personal experience, you will be aware that businesses large and small are regularly faced with all manner of problems from a range of sources – internal and external. In fact, it could be argued that problem solving is the key to business success.

The identification of problems is also a central activity in case study work. Doing a case study analysis requires you to examine a particular business situation in detail and use the skills you have been developing to identify what the key problems are, to identify their causes, to propose appropriate solutions and to evaluate whether these are effective.

Learning outcomes

In this session you will:

- look at the way problems form part of a particular pattern in business texts

- focus more closely on problem identification in case study texts
- organise these problems to suit your purpose
- look at how different framing techniques – including a new one called SWOT – can help this process
- practise using these techniques in writing your own problem analysis.

4.2 What is a problem?

What exactly is a problem? At a basic level, a problem describes a negative situation – a situation which threatens or challenges an individual, a group or an organisation, as in the following scenarios.

Text A

A Following a promotion, a senior administrator is struggling to adapt to the increased pressure of her new and unfamiliar role.

B A newspaper journalist finds the constant noise of the new open-plan office makes it impossible for him to concentrate on his work.

C A middle manager feels undervalued and demotivated after several years in the same job and with little prospect of promotion ahead.

D The threat of redundancy is causing great anxiety among unskilled workers in a distribution warehouse.

4.3 Problems and perception

Yet problems are a matter of perception. One person may perceive a situation as a problem while someone else may be quite satisfied with the same situation. So, while the senior administrator in scenario A is struggling to adapt to the increased pressures of her new job, another person in a similar situation might thrive on the same challenges. Similarly, while the newspaper journalist in scenario B finds the noise levels of the open-plan office distracting to his work, someone else might consider the 'buzz' of this kind of environment energising and productive. In the same way, while the middle manager in scenario C feels undervalued and demotivated, another person could be happy with the routine familiarity of the same work and would not welcome the increased responsibility that a promotion might bring. Similarly, while the threat of redundancy is understandably a concern, particularly if alternative employment opportunities are scarce, people who already had plans to leave, or who were close to retirement, could consider the offer of redundancy pay a welcome bonus.

Whether a situation is considered a problem depends on how it is interpreted. A problem therefore only exists if a person or group of people views it as such.

This is also illustrated in some of the case study texts that you have already read. The 'US Airlines' and 'Chilean Copper Mines' case studies in Sessions 2 and 3 both describe problem-filled situations; but who considers these situations to be problematic? A case study text may present a problematic situation from a single point of view: for example, that of the company director or a particular group of employees. Alternatively, it may present several problems, each perceived as such by a different group of stakeholders.

In addition to these 'insider' views, case study writers often bring their own interpretations to the situation being described. This adds a further perspective to the representation of problems in these texts.

The case study analyses – or output texts – which you write will require you to look in from the *outside* and apply a combination of insights, business knowledge and tools to assess the problematic aspects of a business situation.

4.4 The problem–solution pattern in business texts

Session 1 introduced the idea that written texts are organised differently according to their purpose. Texts about problems and solutions tend to follow a predictable pattern. Being familiar with this pattern will help you read and map these types of text more easily. Similarly, using this pattern to organise your case study write-up will make your writing easier for other people to follow. You will now look at this pattern in detail.

A simple problem–solution text consists of five steps. The following activity will help you identify each step in turn.

Activity 4.1

Purpose: to identify the problem–solution pattern in a case study text.

Task: Text B below is a simple text with a problem–solution pattern. Read the text through once. Then answer the questions following it.

Text B   Presto Pizza

Presto, a pizza delivery company, is expanding rapidly.
However, the pizzas are often cold by the time they are delivered.
This is because there is a shortage of motorcycle delivery riders.
So Presto recruits more motorcycle delivery riders.
As a result, its customers are satisfied.

1   What is the starting situation? What is the text about?

_____

2   What is the problem?

_____

3   What is the cause of the problem?

_____

4   What solution is proposed?

_____

5   Is it successful, in your view?

_____

Compare your answers with those suggested in the Answer section.

Comment

The questions on Text B follow the standard five-step problem–solution. The questions that you answered helped you to map each step in turn (Figure 4.1).

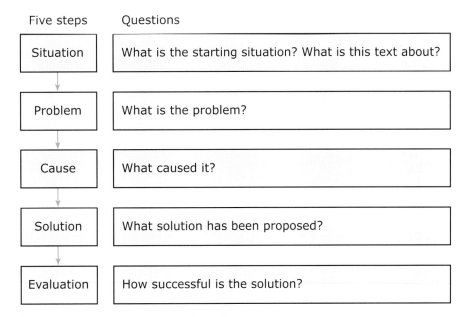

Five steps   Questions

| Situation | What is the starting situation? What is this text about? |

| Problem | What is the problem? |

| Cause | What caused it? |

| Solution | What solution has been proposed? |

| Evaluation | How successful is the solution? |

Figure 4.1   For use with Activity 4.1

The first question asks about the initial **situation**. This looks promising for Presto. The company is expanding rapidly. However, there seems to be a **problem**. The pizzas are often cold by the time customers receive them. In order to solve the problem, the company investigates it further. It decides that the cold pizzas are **caused by** a shortage of delivery drivers. This is the **underlying problem** that needs to be addressed. The company proposes a **solution** – to recruit more drivers. An **evaluation** of the outcome shows that the solution has been successful as the company's customers are now satisfied.

When people or organisations are in a situation which they see as a problem, their natural response is to look for ways of solving it. However, as this scenario shows, this will only be successful if you have established what the underlying problem is that needs to be addressed. This is also true of doing a case study analysis.

Sessions 1 and 2 introduced a set of strategies for reading a text more efficiently. One of these was to ask yourself questions before and while you read. Asking yourself the questions above can help you identify more easily the five main steps of a problem–solution text. You will now use these questions to map the five steps of another text.

Activity 4.2

Purpose: to map the problem–solution pattern in a case study text.

Task: Text C below is about scheduling shift work in a city hospital. Read it through quickly once, then again more carefully, using the five questions to identify the problem–solution pattern. Then copy out the section of text which corresponds to each step in Figure 4.2.

Text C   Scheduling work at Hope City Hospital

Hope City Hospital employs over 2000 staff who provide 24-hour care on a shift basis. The scheduling of work shifts for this number of people has always been a source of contention because people are not consulted about their preferences.

The human resource department has recently introduced a new schedule, which involves three eight-hour shifts from Monday to Friday and two 12-hour shifts at the weekends. The advantage of this schedule is its predictability. Because employees know exactly when they will be working, they can plan their non-working hours around their shifts.

(Adapted from Cherrington, 1995, p. 81)

Five steps

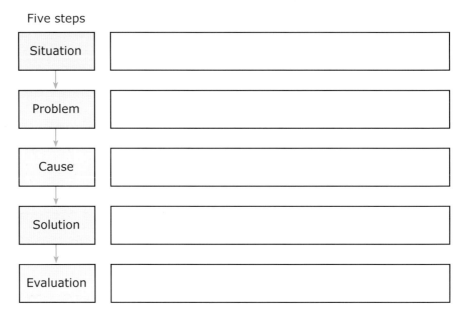

Figure 4.2   For use with Activity 4.2

Compare your answers with those suggested in the Answer section.

Comment

Although this text contains more information than the Presto Pizza one, it has the same pattern. There are two sentences for the **evaluation** step, but all the others have just one sentence.

Mapping a longer problem–solution text

Texts B and C above are short texts which can be mapped line-by-line onto the problem–solution pattern. However, with longer texts, it is unlikely that every line can be mapped in this way.

Session 1 introduced the technique of mapping a text by identifying its main ideas, or high-level generalisations, which were summarised concisely in the form of key concept notes. This note-making strategy can also be used to summarise the pattern of a problem–solution text. You will practise using this technique in the next activity.

Activity 4.3 ....

Purpose: to use key concepts to identify the steps in a longer problem–solution case text.

Task: Text 4.1, 'From competition to collaboration', in Resource Book 1 is about staffing problems in the electronics industry. Read through it quickly to get an idea of its content. Then, using the five questions as a guide, match the five steps in the left-hand column with the correct word group in the right-hand column of Figure 4.3.

Five steps

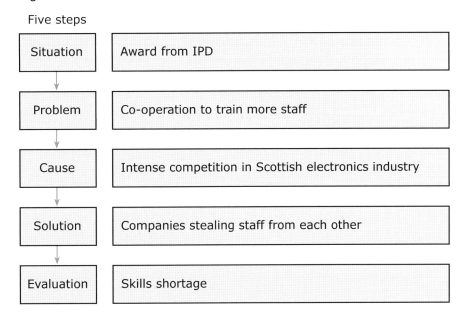

Situation	Award from IPD
Problem	Co-operation to train more staff
Cause	Intense competition in Scottish electronics industry
Solution	Companies stealing staff from each other
Evaluation	Skills shortage

Figure 4.3 For use with Activity 4.3

Compare your answers with those suggested in the Answer section.

Comment ....

In Session 1 you learned how to map a case by seeing the levels in a text. Texts move up and down between high level generalisations and lower-level details and examples. This is a general–particular pattern. Activity 4.3 shows another pattern. This time you have identified the problem–solution pattern. These two patterns work together. The key concepts in the problem–solution pattern are often high-level generalisations as well.

This activity demonstrates that there are no rules about the length of each step of a problem–solution text. Any one may range from a single sentence to several paragraphs or pages. You will see later that sometimes the steps are presented in a different order from the standard sequence here. You will also see that, with more complex texts, the steps may not be so self-contained. For example, where there is more than one problem, they may be referred to in different parts of the text. You will look at this more closely in Section 4.9.

Review

The first part of this session has introduced a new text pattern – one that is commonly used in writing about problems and solutions. The problem–solution pattern is valuable in analysing a business case for three reasons:

- It can help you **read** a case study text by providing you with a pattern to guide you in mapping and then summarising its main steps in the form of key concept notes.

- It can help you **analyse** a case study text by helping you focus on the problem.

- It provides a model to follow when you **write up** your case study analysis. (This is the focus of Sessions 5 and 6).

From now on this session focuses more specifically on the **problem** step of this pattern.

4.5 Noticing problem language

As you have seen, whether a situation is considered a problem depends on how it is interpreted. The interpretation of the situation is reflected in the words used to describe it. This is illustrated in each of the scenarios that you read in Text A. The way in which these scenarios are written makes it clear that each is a problem for those involved. Now look more closely at what makes this so.

Signal words

You have already been introduced to the notion of signal words or phrases in a text. You saw examples of words which are commonly associated with defining and categorising in Session 2 and identified others signalling influences and impacts in Session 3.

Problem-signalling words

The fact that you were able to identify the problem step of the problem–solution texts that you read earlier shows that you noticed the words and phrases sending the message 'this is a problem!' as you were reading.

Look again at the problem scenarios in Text A at the beginning of this session. They contain several words and phrases which signal 'this is a problem!' The first one that jumps out is the word *struggling* in scenario A. Can you spot any more? Compare them with the list below.

struggling	undervalued
increased pressure	demotivated
unfamiliar	little prospect of promotion
constant noise	threat of redundancy
impossible	great anxiety

All these words and phrases suggest a negative, difficult or challenging situation for the people involved.

Activity 4.4   ....

Purpose: to note the problem-signalling words in another problem text.

Task: Text D describes a problem situation in a factory. Read through it once. Then read it again, underlining any problem-signalling words and expressions that you find. Now copy them out in the space below. The first one is done for you.

Text D   Duplex tyre factory

Duplex tyre factory has been unsuccessful in recruiting sufficient staff. Its existing employees have therefore been expected to take on more work. Increased feelings of exploitation have resulted in a noticeable drop in morale. Productivity per worker is down, while levels of absenteeism are the highest in two years.

Explanations for the recruitment problems include limited public transport links to the factory, low hourly wages as compared with a competitor and a poor health and safety record.

---

unsuccessful

Compare your answers with those suggested in the Answer section.

Positive words and expressions

Texts A and D were only about problems and the focus was on noticing problem-signalling language. However, when you mapped out the five steps of the problem–solution texts earlier, you were also looking out for the **positive** words and expressions which signalled the solution step. An example is the word *advantage* in Text C. Positive words can often be found in other parts of a text too. For example, the words *expanding rapidly* in the first line of Text B indicate that there were positive aspects to this situation. It is important to be alert to the positive aspects of a problem situation when doing a case study analysis, as you will see later in this session.

Activity 4.5   ....

Purpose: to identify the words that signal the problem and those that signal the solution in a familiar text.

Task: this task requires you to look back at Text 4.1, 'From competition to collaboration', in Resource Book 1. Read it again and list both the problem-signalling words and the solution-signalling words in the respective boxes below.

Problem-signalling words and expressions:

Solution-signalling words and expressions:

Compare your answers with those suggested in the Answer section.

Comment

Many words and expressions can be used to signal a problem. Noticing these signal words will help you when reading a case study. Similarly, you can guide your readers by using signal words when you write a case study analysis. You have now recorded several examples of problem-signalling words and expressions. You are advised to record these in MyStuff and that you add further examples as you meet them in your reading.

Some words and expressions may be considered **intrinsically negative** – in that they always signal some kind of problem. Examples of these include *struggling*, *impossible*, *unsuccessful*, *great anxiety*, *threat of redundancy*, *getting out of hand*. These are perhaps the easiest ones to spot.

Other problems are signalled **indirectly**. For example, when **positive things decrease** (for example *productivity is down*) or **negative things increase** (for example *levels of absenteeism are the highest in two years*), this usually indicates a problem.

However, what is perceived as **positive** and what as **negative** can also be a matter of interpretation. This is illustrated by the expression *pushing salaries up* in Text 4.1. From the point of view described in that text – that of the employers – this increase in salaries signals a problem. However, if the situation were described from a different perspective – that of the workers receiving the increased salaries – the same words would probably not be problem-signalling as such increases would most likely be considered to be positive from their point of view.

Note that signal words and phrases are those that catch a reader's attention and alert them to the presence of something significant in the text. They rarely provide enough information on their own. It is usually necessary to read the piece of text in which they occur more carefully to get a full picture of what they refer to.

4.6 Problems, influences and impacts

Whether in everyday life or in business, instead of a single problem there is often a 'problem area' consisting of several, possibly interrelated problems. At times it is difficult to distinguish between the problem itself and the symptoms – or effects – of that problem. What is first identified as the main problem may in fact be the effect of a more fundamental problem. Problems are therefore closely related to the notions of influences and impacts or cause and effect which you studied in Session 3.

This is illustrated in Text D above.

Activity 4.6 ....

Purpose: to consider the relationship between problems, influences and impacts or causes and effects in a sample scenario.

Task: Text D describes a scenario which contains several interrelated problems. Read it again and underline the problems it contains. In note form, complete the flow diagram in Figure 4.4 to show how these problems are related. Now label the boxes with the letters **C**, **E** or **C/E**, depending on which problem is a cause (**C**), which is an effect (**E**) and which is both cause and effect (**C/E**).

In your view, which problem(s) should be addressed first?

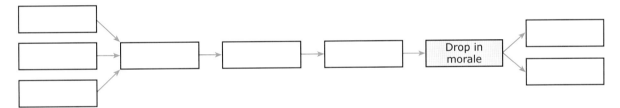

Figure 4.4 For use with Activity 4.6

Compare your answers with those suggested in the Answer section.

Comment ....

This activity demonstrates the way in which problems map closely onto the notions of influences and impacts. It shows that problems are often interrelated. This can take several forms as was illustrated in Figure 3.1 in Session 3. A causal chain is when one problem causes another problem, which in turn causes a further problem, and so on. Sometimes a single problem is the cause of several separate problems. Alternatively, several separate problems may together contribute to the creation of a single new problem.

Figure 4.5 shows that it would be most logical to begin by addressing the three problems which underlie the causal chain, namely limited public transport to the company, low hourly wages as compared with a competitor and a poor health and safety record.

Although the ideal would be to give equal priority to resolving these three underlying problems, the reality of both business and every-day situations is that choices often have to be made about which problem(s) to address first. The relative cost of addressing the problem, the complexity of doing this, the immediacy and level of impact this is likely to have plus others factors need to be taken into account when making such decisions.

It could be argued that, of the three underlying problems listed above, improving transport arrangements to and from the factory, by providing a mini-bus service or offering incentives for car sharing, may be the easiest and cheapest to implement. However, it must also be recognised that, while addressing this cause may improve the situation, attending to it alone is unlikely to be sufficient to fully resolve it.

4.7 Analysing the problems in a case study text

So far this session has been concerned with **noticing** and **mapping** problems as they appear in a case study text. However, a problem-oriented assignment will require you to do more than this. For example, you will be asked to use business concepts to organise these problems, to prioritise them in order of importance or to establish which problem underlies the others. It is difficult to see the complexities of a particular problem-filled situation without a systematic approach to its analysis.

Here are some examples of the types of problem-oriented assignment questions that you might encounter.

1   Using the stakeholder model of business environments, examine the factors external to the company which contributed to Enron's eventual downfall.

2   Sam Potts's changes in the business appear to be based on moving from one type of business structure to another. Describe the two types of structure, using appropriate concepts, and then write about the problems and benefits that might ensue in moving from one to the other.

3   Given the differing historic and cultural contexts of Napster and Bertelsmann, what are the most important inter- and intra-organisational problems that might be expected to emerge in the first few years of their merger?

4   Critically evaluate the benefits and any disadvantages of the organisational arrangements in the case study for managing these business functions: marketing, operations, human resource management, accounting and finance, and information management.

5   What can Stuart do to alleviate some of the performance problems the team is facing?

As you can see, very often the question specifies or strongly indicates the business concepts that would be most suitable for the problem analysis.

Using frameworks to categorise or organise problems

You have encountered several business frameworks in this book so far, among them **STEP** and **stakeholder analysis**. Both of these are closely connected to the notions of influences and impacts or cause and effect and so to the analysis of problems.

STEP is concerned with examining the environmental influences which impact on a business. Some of these may be positive; others may be problematic. A STEP framework can therefore be useful in identifying the problems in a case study text. However, because STEP only picks up the problems that are caused by the factors that are **external** to a business, it will not necessarily be sufficient in helping you identify **all** of the problems the organisation is facing. Some of these problems may be caused by **internal** factors, so you will need to apply another analytical tool or framework to identify these as well.

As mentioned above, it is also important to notice the **positive** aspects of a problem situation. A STEP analysis can help you identify the factors in the environment that impact positively on a company as well.

A stakeholder analysis, in turn, is concerned with assessing the relative levels of *power* and *interest* of the people connected with a business. Any change that is introduced must be carefully considered in terms of its effect on those with power or interest; a negative impact translating into a potential problem for the organisation. Similarly, when dealing with existing problems, decisions about how best to resolve them will often depend on the potential reactions of stakeholders.

Unfortunately, there is no single framework that highlights all the problems in a case study text. As was mentioned above, an assignment title may indicate which framework is most suitable for a particular purpose. Alternatively, you may have to make this decision yourself. Sometimes it will be appropriate to apply more than one analytical framework to a problem situation to get several perspectives on the case. Some of the student assignments you saw in previous sessions did this.

It should be mentioned that your personal insights and experience are always an important additional factor, whatever framework(s) you use in a case study analysis.

The SWOT framework

You will now look at another framework called SWOT. This acronym stands for Strengths, Weaknesses, Opportunities and Threats. A SWOT analysis is a means of getting an overview of how an organisation is functioning at a particular point in time. Therefore, it can provide another way of categorising an organisation's problems.

Activity 4.7   ....

Purpose: to become familiar with the components of a SWOT analysis.

Task: read the paragraphs below and complete the heading above each one according to whether it is describing strengths, weaknesses, opportunities or threats.

1

These are the areas in which an organisation lacks the necessary qualities or attributes required to perform better than its competitors.

2

> In order to gain advantages over its competitors, an organisation must be alert to the potential openings available in its external environment, by breaking new ground, developing its products and services or expanding its scale of operation in order to gain more customers.

3

> These are those aspects of the external environment that could harm an organisation's performance. They often arise from the actions of competitors or factors outside the control of the organisation.

4

> These are the distinctive qualities, resources or reputation of a business or an organisation – any feature which gives it an advantage over its competitors. They represent a company's greatest weapon.

Now complete the following paragraph.

> In general, in order to succeed, an organisation needs to aim to be better than its competitors when it comes to possessing _____ and exploring _____ , while at the same time minimising the effect of its _____ and _____ to a greater extent than its competitors.

Compare your answers with those suggested in the Answer section.

Comment   ....

The identification of a company's strengths, weaknesses, opportunities and threats can be based on subjective judgement or on formal analysis using a range of business concepts to frame the analysis.

Using SWOT with everyday business situations

You will now see how SWOT can be applied to a business situation. There are two main uses of SWOT, as outlined in the following sections.

The first way is to apply it to an everyday business situation with which you are familiar. This use of SWOT requires you to draw on your experience or perceptions of that organisation to brainstorm and list what you consider to be its strengths, weaknesses, opportunities and threats at a particular point in time.

Some organisations use SWOT in this way as an occasional group brainstorming and discussion tool with sections of their staff. This kind of activity can provide valuable insights into the internal perceptions of both the positive and negative aspects of the organisation, while stimulating the generation of ideas for how it might be improved.

Below is an example of this kind of analysis, as applied to a handmade shoe manufacturer where one of the authors once worked.

Strengths	Weaknesses
Long-established company Large proportion of return customers Prestige central London address Recognised leader in field in terms of staff training opportunities	Labour-intensive, individually made, high-cost products Some production processes not environmentally friendly. Personal fitting service means opportunities for mail order and online ordering and distribution are very limited Building cramped and poorly ventilated
Opportunities	**Threats**
Increasing recognition of value of niche market – as opposed to mass-produced –goods. Potential for increased publicity in connection with 150th anniversary of business	Increasing cheapness of mass-produced shoes Return customers generally older, not being replaced by new customers when they die Some staff leaving to set up own businesses with high fashion competing products Lease on building due to expire – risk that it may be too expensive to renew in similar location Increase in cost of raw materials

Activity 4.8 ....

Purpose: to practise applying SWOT to an everyday business situation.

Task: you will now do your own SWOT analysis, based on a business or an organisation with which you are familiar. It may be somewhere you currently work or have worked in the past. If you don't have work experience, you can base the analysis on what someone else tells you about where they work.

Using a grid similar to the one above, complete each section with your ideas in note form as follows.

- First, list what you consider to be the **strengths** of the business.
- Does the business have any **weaknesses**, in your view? If so, note them down.
- Now consider what kinds of **threats** the business might face.
- Finally, note down any **opportunities** that could be available to it. What possibilities are there for it to develop and become more successful?

4.8 Using SWOT with a case study text

The second way in which SWOT can be used is to analyse a written case study. Here completion of the SWOT grid will be based on your interpretation of the evidence in the input texts that you are drawing on for the purpose of your analysis.

You will practise doing this in the next activity.

The activity is based on a newspaper article about the soft-drinks manufacturer Coca-Cola.

Activity 4.9 ....

Purpose: to practise applying SWOT to a case study text.

Task: read quickly through Text 4.2 in Resource Book 1. Then read it again more carefully and consider which factors would be considered strengths, weaknesses, opportunities and threats for the Coca-Cola company. Complete the grid below with your notes. Some of it is already done for you.

A SWOT analysis of Coca-Cola

Strengths	Weaknesses
World-recognised brand	Uncertainty from internal restructuring
Opportunities	**Threats**
Vanilla-flavoured drink – biggest innovation in 20 years?	More health-conscious customers – decrease in sales

Compare your answers with those suggested in the Answer section.

Comment ....

Writing up a SWOT analysis

A common business studies task is to write up the SWOT analysis that you have done on a case study text.

Text 4.3 in Resource Book 1 is an example of a student's write-up of the completed SWOT analysis on Coca-Cola.

Activity 4.10 ....

Purpose: to examine how a SWOT analysis is usually written up.

Task: read Text 4.3 through once and then again more carefully and answer the questions below.

1   What information is included in the introductory sentence?
2   What is covered by the next four paragraphs?
3   How is the topic of each paragraph introduced?
4   What else is included in each of these four paragraphs?

Compare your answers with those suggested in the Answer section.

Comment ....

Some additional comments are included in the Answer section.

4.9 SWOT and organising business problems

How does a SWOT analysis help to categorise and organise the problems of a business? As you have seen, a SWOT analysis provides a frame for focusing on four different aspects of a business situation, some of which may be considered positive, some more problematic. A SWOT analysis can also help to identify which of the problematic aspects are likely to be easier to address, as the next activity demonstrates.

Activity 4.11 ....

Purpose: to examine the categories of SWOT more closely.

Task: look back at the description of the four SWOT categories in Activity 4.7 (Strengths, Weaknesses, Opportunities, Threats) and answer the questions below.

- Which of these categories would be expected to have a positive impact on a business?
- Which categories would be expected to have a negative impact on a business?
- Which are internal to a business?
- Which are external to a business?

Note these in the grid below.

Impact	Internal to the business	External to the business
Positive		
Negative		

When you have completed the grid:

- Highlight the categories which a business is most likely to be able to control.
- Draw a box round the categories which a business is most likely to consider problematic.

Compare your answers with those suggested in the Answer section.

Comment ....

A SWOT analysis is a way of identifying the forces that impact on an organisation either positively or negatively and those that are either internal or external to it. In this way it is a categorising framework which separates elements into four different groups.

Activity 4.11 shows that weaknesses and threats both represent problems to an organisation. However, in general, the forces **inside** an organisation are easier to control, influence or alter than those **outside**. This suggests that a business will have more success in trying to address its internal weaknesses than its external threats. In terms of **prioritising** problems, the problems in the **weaknesses** section should therefore be addressed first.

(Note too that weaknesses are closely related to the notion of the **operating environment** while threats are related to the notion of the **far environment** – both of which you met in Session 2.)

4.10 Working with longer texts with multiple problems

Most case study input texts are like the Coca-Cola one in that they have several problems dispersed throughout them. As you saw earlier in this session, initially it may not be obvious how problems interact in terms of impacts and influences or cause and effect or how best to organise them to establish which to address first.

This section will guide you through the process of doing a problem analysis.

The problem analysis is based on the following assignment question.

What factors have contributed to the decline in Gap's business profits?

A Gap store in the United States

First reading

As with all text-based tasks, the first step is to read the text to get an overview of its content. Use the strategies that you learned in Session 1 for this purpose.

Activity 4.12

Purpose: to get an overview of the content of a longer text

Task: in Text 3.2 read through the section 'Gap goes into decline?'. Find the words and expressions that mean the same as those listed below.

unaffected	continuous
get through the crisis	dull
support	principal components
following	list of items in stock
clothing	mistakes
caused (by)	casual cotton tops with a hood

Compare your answers with those suggested in the Answer section.

Listing problems

When working with longer texts containing multiple problems, a valuable first step is to list all the problems you can find.

Having read the extract through once, go back and read it again more carefully, making a list of the problems as you do so. You will find that being alert to problem-signalling words will help you in this process. At this stage, it is sufficient simply to list the problems in the order that you meet them in the text. You will organise and analyse them later.

Activity 4.13

Purpose: to list the problems in a case study text.

Task: read the section of Text 3.2 again, focusing on the problem-signalling words as you do so. Make a list of all the problems that you find in the text, capturing each of them in the form of key concept notes.

Compare your answers with those suggested in the Answer section.

Comment

There is no precise answer to this listing activity. Text 3.2 is typical of a longer case study text. It has many problems distributed throughout it. Sometimes what seems to be the same problem is mentioned more than once in slightly different words, such as the references to both *a decline in sales* and *disappointing sales* in paragraph one (or *consumer nervousness/loss of confidence* in paragraphs 2 and 3). The different voices or perspectives of stakeholders and analysts mentioned in the text can add to this confusion. An example of this is the reference to *criticisms of Gap's confused brand identity*, followed by the quotation '*we lost sight of our brand positioning*' a little later in the text. Another complicating factor is that what may be presented as an underlying problem early on in the text is later shown not to be the case. Thus, while the general economic slowdown was initially blamed for Gap's decline in sales, the company later accepted that other – internal – problems were the main reasons for its difficulties.

Organising problems: cause and effect

Having made a list of the problems in the section of Text 3.2, the next stage is to organise them in some way.

Section 4.6 explained how a problem situation often consists of several interrelated problems and how, by establishing the causal relationship between them, you will be in a better position to know which problem(s) should be prioritised for attention.

Activity 4.14

Purpose: to draw a diagram or concept map of the problems in 'Gap goes into decline?' showing any cause-effect relationships that occur between them.

Task: using the list of problems from Activity 4.9, and the original text for reference, draw a simple diagram or concept map of the problems in this case study. Where there are causal links between them, indicate this by the letters **C** (cause), **E** (effect) and **C/E** (cause–effect) as appropriate.

Compare your answer with the one suggested in the Answer section.

Comment

Once again, there is no definitive way of presenting this kind of information. Some of the relationships between the problems in the case will be open to interpretation. By organising problems according to their causal relationship in this way, you will gain one perspective on which one(s) would be most usefully addressed.

Organising problems: SWOT

An alternative way of organising the problems in 'Gap goes into decline?' is to do a SWOT analysis of the case study text. You should recall from Activity 4.11 that the problem areas of an organisation are normally associated with the **weaknesses** and **threats** categories of a SWOT analysis. For this reason, it is only necessary to complete those two sections in the next activity.

Activity 4.15

Purpose: to do a SWOT analysis on a case study text.

Task: read again through the list you made of problems you noted when reading 'Gap goes into decline?'.

Which of these factors would be considered weaknesses? Which would be considered threats? Complete the grid below with your notes. Remember that, because you are only focusing on the company's problems, you don't need to complete the strengths and opportunities categories of the SWOT grid.

An example is already provided for you.

Strengths	Weaknesses
	Uninspiring merchandise
Opportunities	**Threats**

Compare your answers with those suggested in the Answer section.

Comment ....

As with the full SWOT analyses you did earlier, an analysis of the weaknesses and threats in the case study text will be somewhat subjective and open to your personal interpretation of the situation.

However, categorising Gap's problems into internal and external factors in this way provides another perspective on which to prioritise first.

4.11 Writing up a problem analysis

The final stage in identifying and organising problems is to produce a write-up of your problem analysis.

Text 4.4 in Resource Book 1 is a student's write-up of their answer to the question 'What factors have contributed to the decline in Gap's business profits?'

This is considered a successful assignment. What features contribute to this? You will consider this in the next activity.

Activity 4.16 ....

Purpose: to notice the constituents of a successful problem analysis by a student.

Task: read Text 4.4 in Resource Book 1 and – by underlining and circling examples and making notes in the margin – identify all the features that it contains, as follows.

- Brief reference to type of company under discussion
- Reference to assignment question
- Examples of cause–effect relationships between problems
- Reference to weaknesses with examples
- References to threats with examples from the case study texts
- References to different people's views
- Linking words showing the direction of the text (find examples of these)
- Summing up of analysis
- Personal judgement

Commentary on the write-up

One or two points should be made about the write-up of a problem analysis such as that for Gap.

First, the identification of Gap's weaknesses and threats is based on a range of different perspectives in the input text. These include company executives, spokespeople and analysts. At times it is not clear whether the views cited by one of these groups are shared by the others. Moreover, just because an analyst considers an aspect of the business to be a weakness, for example, does not automatically make it so. Therefore, it is important to make it clear whose opinion is being cited when reporting opinions in this way.

Yet the most important perspective of all in a written-up analysis of this kind is **yours** as the writer–analyst. A good write-up will combine the writer-analyst's framing and interpretation of a situation with evidence and examples from the input text.

Second, normally a SWOT analysis is based on input material which provides a snapshot of a company at a particular point in time (as was the case with the Coca-Cola text). A complicating factor for the analysis above is that, instead of a snapshot, the case study material reports Gap's business developments over a period of time, during which it undergoes several changes.

4.12 Writing your own problem analysis

Businesses are necessarily dynamic, evolving entities. The next text that you will read is a newspaper article which contains an update on developments within Gap. This will form the input text of the comprehensive problem analysis that you will now do, drawing on the techniques that you have learned so far in this book.

Activity 4.17   ....

Purpose: to do a problem analysis, write it up and post it online.

Task: compare the update on Gap (Text 4.5) with the description of the company some five years earlier ('Gap goes into decline?' in Text 3.2).

What problems is the company facing in the updated text? To what extent are they the same as those in the earlier text? In what ways are they different?

There is no single way of approaching this task. The following guidelines are based on the procedures you have followed in this session. However, you may want to do them in a different order or skip a stage.

- Read the input text (Text 4.5) to get an overview of its content, using the mapping techniques you learned in Session 1.
- Read Text 4.5 again, focusing on the problem-signalling words as you do so.
- Make a list of all the problems that you find in the text, capturing each of them in the form of key concept notes.
- Draw a cause-and-effect diagram showing the relationships between the problems in the case study text.
- Using a grid template, do a partial SWOT analysis of the text, focusing on its problems – namely, the weaknesses and threats categories.
- Compare the analyses of 'Gap goes into decline?' (Text 3.2) with those you did on Text 4.5 and use these as the basis for planning your write-up in response to the question above.

4.13 Critical reflection

Write some notes in your Learning Journal on the different skills you drew on from Sessions 1–4 in completing your problem analysis in Activity 4.17.

4.14 Vocabulary activity

See the course website for how to do a vocabulary-building activity for this session.

4.15 Review

In this session you have:

- developed your understanding of the way problems form part of a particular pattern in business texts
- developed skills of identifying problems in case study texts
- learned how to organise these problems in order to suit your purpose
- learned how different framing techniques – including a new one called SWOT – can help this process
- developed skills in using these techniques to write your own problem analysis.

4.16 Answer section

Activity 4.1

1 Presto is a pizza delivery company that is expanding rapidly.
2 Its pizzas are often cold.
3 A shortage of delivery drivers.
4 To recruit more drivers.
5 Yes: its customers are now satisfied.

Activity 4.2

1 Situation: Hope City Hospital employs over 2000 staff who provide 24-hour care on a shift basis.
2 Problem: the scheduling of work shifts for this number of people has always been a source of contention.
3 Cause: people are not consulted about their shift work preferences.
4 Solution: the human resource department has recently introduced a new schedule, which involves three eight-hour shifts from Monday to Friday and two 12-hour shifts at the weekends.
5 Evaluation: the advantage of this schedule is its predictability: because employees know exactly when they will be working, they can plan their non-working hours around their shifts.

Activity 4.3

1 Situation: intense competition in Scottish electronics industry
2 Problem: competing companies pushing up salaries
3 Cause: skills shortage
4 Solution: cooperation to train more staff
5 Evaluation: award from IPD

Activity 4.4

The problem-signalling words and expressions in Text D are as follows.

unsuccessful
increased feelings of exploitation
drop in morale
productivity – down
levels of absenteeism highest in two years.
limited transport links
low hourly wages
poor health and safety record

Activity 4.5

The problem-signalling words and expressions in Text 4.1 are as follows.

> famously intense
> recruitment problems
> salaries pushed up
> getting out of hand
> a vicious circle

The solution-signalling words and expressions in Text 4.1 are as follows.

> in a striking turnaround
> an unprecedented degree of cooperation
> their innovative approach was recognised
> they received a special training award

Activity 4.6

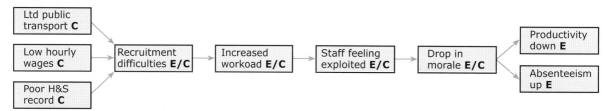

Figure 4.5 Causal links between the problems in the Duplex tyre factory

Ideally, all three underlying causes of the above chain – namely, limited public transport to the factory, low hourly wages, and a poor health and safety record – should be addressed in order to solve the recruitment difficulties which are responsible for creating further problems in the chain.

See the comment on this activity for more discussion about this point.

Activity 4.7

1   Weaknesses
2   Opportunities
3   Threats
4   Strengths

Activity 4.9

Strengths	Weaknesses
World-recognised brand	Uncertainty from internal restructuring
Sponsorship of winter Olympics	Share price has halved since 1998
Largest market share at 43.7%	
Development and improved sales of diet product	
Renewed confidence in Coca-Cola	

Opportunities	Threats
Vanilla-flavoured drink – biggest innovation in 20 years?	More health-conscious customers – decrease in sales
Move into the bottled-water market	Slight decrease in market share for Coke
Possibilities of further world sponsorship opportunities	Development by Pepsi of diet product
	Increase in market share by Pepsi
	Increase in popularity of bottled water
	Pepsi number 2 in bottled-water market

Activity 4.10

1   The introductory sentence includes a reference to: the <u>analysis</u> being undertaken (in this case SWOT), the <u>organisation</u> it is being applied to (Coca-Cola), and to the <u>case study</u> which forms the input text.

2   Paragraphs 2 to 5 cover strengths, weaknesses, threats and opportunities in turn. Note that there is no fixed order, but it is common to start with strengths and weaknesses, while threats and opportunities may be introduced in either order.

3   The <u>first sentence</u> (topic sentence) of each paragraph introduces the category being described in that section.

4   Specific examples of strengths, weaknesses, opportunities and threats from the case study are transferred to the grid.

Note that this student has also included some of her own interpretations and additional knowledge of Coca-Cola. However, this is not generally a requirement of a written-up SWOT analysis.

Activity 4.11

Impact	Internal to the business	External to the business
Positive	**Strengths**	Opportunities
Negative	**[Weaknesses]**	[Threats]

Activity 4.12

unaffected	unscathed
continuous	sustained
get through the crisis	weather the storm
dull	uninspiring
support	backing
principal components	basics
following	in the wake of
list of items in stock	inventory
clothing	apparel
mistakes	screw-ups
caused (by)	sparked (by)
casual cotton tops with a hood	hoodies

Activity 4.13

- Serious decline in sales
- Drop in profits
- Fall in share prices
- General economic slowdown in the USA
- Slump in the stock market
- Rises in interest rates
- High levels of US consumer debt
- Elections
- Consumer nervousness
- Uninspiring merchandise
- Poor management
- Bad weather
- Inventory problems
- Moving away from or losing sight of core business – strengths – brand positioning
- Confused brand identity or loss of focus

Activity 4.14

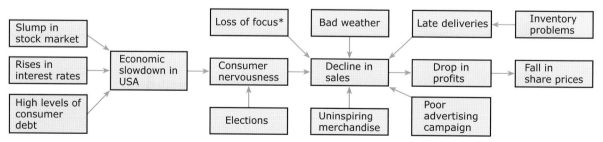

Figure 4.6   Concept map of problems in Gap

Activity 4.15

Strengths	Weaknesses
	Uninspiring merchandise
	Poor management
	Inventory problems leading to late deliveries
	Dispiriting advertising campaign
	Confused brand identity/loss of focus
	Moving away from core business/customers

Opportunities	Threats
	Economic slowdown in USA – caused by:
	slump in stock market
	rise in interest rates
	high levels of US consumer debt
	Elections – making consumers nervous – affecting clothes sales
	Bad weather

SESSION 5 Proposing solutions

5.1 Introduction

In Session 4 you focused on the problem part of the problem–solution pattern. In this session, you will look at how to propose solutions for these problems. You may recall that the problem–solution pattern is a series of questions. What is the problem? What is the cause? What is the solution? It is as if problems are questions which are looking for answers. In fact, this is what people say in everyday conversation – 'Have you got an answer to the problem?' – and in business discussions, after a long analysis of the problems, it is not unusual to hear a manager say something like, 'Let's stop talking about problems and hear some solutions.'

Many case study assignments expect the same. Sometimes they are quite direct about it and it is obvious they want you to solve problems:

> **What can Stuart do to solve some of the problems the team is facing? What actions would you recommend him to take and why?**

Sometimes they are not so direct but the answer still involves problem solving:

> **Describe the two types of business structure, using appropriate concepts, and then write about the problems and benefits that might ensue in moving from one to the other.**

In this session, the activities are based on a single case study assignment. This has been chosen because the whole assignment is a solution to a problem. It contains many examples of the communication skills you need for problem solving. However, this session does not attempt to deal with every skill needed for problem solving. You should also remember that in many case study assignments, problem solving is part of a longer analysis.

Learning outcomes

In this session you will:

- examine the language and organisation of problem-solving assignments
- look at some of the input texts that students read to find solutions
- practise problem-solving processes
- write a solution text.

5.2 Solutions: input text 1

As you may recall from Session 3, Gap received some negative publicity for being involved in 'sweat shops'. Some factories making Gap garments were paying very low wages. When you read the extract about this previously, it was framed by the stakeholder concept. This time, the assignment question asks students to frame their analysis with a different concept. In the first activity you will simply concentrate on what happened in the extract from the case study. At the end of the activity you will see the question that students were asked to frame their analysis of this case.

Activity 5.1 ....

Purpose: to map the case study.

Task 1: the text has been divided into four extracts. At the beginning of each extract there are some statements about it and at the end there is a vocabulary activity. First, look quickly through the extract. Then read it more carefully and decide which of the statements are true. Finally, do the vocabulary activity. There is a full version of this case study in Resource Book 1 (the fourth section of Text 3.2).

Extract A

Statements

1 Gap clothing is produced in 3000 Gap factories.
2 The companies that make Gap clothes are called vendors.
3 Gap does not pay much attention to quality and production standards in vendor companies.
4 The Code of Vendor Conduct deals with ethical standards among vendors.

Sourcing of manufactured goods

Despite having what they claim is a 'global reach', Gap do not own or operate any factories for the manufacture of garments. In 2002 their clothing was produced in around 3000 factories in over 50 countries. They claim that 'Sourcing our product with a variety of vendors gives greater flexibility when fashion dictates the use of different fabrics, techniques or expertise' ('Beyond the Label' fact sheet from Gap.com). This international network of manufacturers is controlled via rigorous processes of prior vetting and monitoring against company standards. Some of these standards relate to quality assurance and production engineering – ensuring that a manufacturer meets the required quality standards and has the capacity to accept a particular order – while others relate to Gap's corporate ethical values. The framework for this is set out in a Code of Vendor Conduct which Gap first produced in the early 1990s in response to criticisms of 'sweat shop' labour conditions amongst some of its vendors.

Vocabulary

For each word below on the left, decide which of the four words on the right is the most similar in meaning.

sourcing	manufacturing, obtaining, vetting, monitoring
vendor	buyer, inspector, supplier, flexibility
ethical values	framework, production quality, code of conduct, global reach
vetting	producing, owning, controlling, inspecting

Extract B

Statements

1 The factory in Saipan was an example of a 'sweat shop'.
2 Gap knew about the situation in this factory before the American reporter published the story.
3 The Code of Vendor Conduct introduced baby-friendly quiet rooms into Pacific clothing factories.

As the *Guardian* later published:

'The shine was first tarnished in 1992, when an American reporter stumbled upon a factory in Saipan, in the Pacific, where Gap clothes were being produced by a subcontractor who, unknown to Gap, was hiring Chinese labourers for 80-hour weeks at less than $2 an hour. The company quickly denounced and sacked the contractor, but this was still unwelcome publicity for an organisation with native grasses planted on the roof of its San Francisco headquarters for eco-friendly insulation, and baby-friendly quiet rooms for nursing mothers.' (*The Guardian*, 23/11/01). As a result Gap Inc. produced the Code as a means of influencing working conditions and management practices in their vendor organizations.

Vocabulary

For each word below on the left, decide which of the four words on the right is the most similar in meaning.

subcontractor	supplier, manufacturer, organisation, management
working conditions	management practices, publicity, vendor organisations, rate of pay

Extract C

Statements

1 The Global Compliance Team is part of the Vendor Compliance Team.

2 Their main task is enforcing corrective action on health and safety.

3 Their goal is to ensure that vendor organisations are culturally the same as Gap.

4 If the vendor does not improve, the Vendor Compliance Officers terminate business with the vendor.

The monitoring and evaluation of Gap-approved garment producers is conducted by a multinational team of Vendor Compliance Officers (VCOs) who are part of Gap Inc.'s Global Compliance Team based in San Francisco. They are drawn from a variety of backgrounds such as the law, academia and the voluntary sector. Their role encompasses a range of activities including conducting routine site visits, investigations of reported breaches of the Code, enforcing corrective action on health and safety, acting as advocate for a vendor's employee and negotiating improvement programmes with vendors. Their objective is to ensure Gap Inc.'s vendor organizations understand the company's ethical commitments and that they abide by them as closely as possible allowing for differences in cultural context. Gap's approach is to encourage continuous improvement but where serious breaches of the Code of Conduct or a pattern of non-compliance occur, they suspend or terminate business with the vendor. In 2002 they terminated business with vendors owning 120 factories around the world.

Vocabulary

For each word or phrase below on the left, decide which of the four words on the right is the most similar in meaning.

to comply with	to understand, to allow for, to terminate, to abide by
commitments	principles, agreements, investigations, improvements
breaches of the code	improvements of the code, breaking of the code, termination of the code, investigations of the code

Extract D

Statements

1 The vendor selection and monitoring process was successful.

2 Africa Forum and Unite supported the vendor monitoring process.

3 The only problems were long hours and health hazards.

Despite this, the company came in for renewed criticism from development campaigners in 2002. The campaign group Africa Forum joined together with Unite, the international union of textile workers, to publicise and denounce what they saw as 'abusive working conditions' – a combination of long hours, low pay, health hazards and exploitative management practice – amongst Gap's suppliers in at least six countries. In a press release the campaigners called for a consumer boycott during the run-up to Christmas 2002.

Vocabulary

For each word or phrase below on the left, decide which of the four words on the right is the most similar in meaning.

abusive	renewed, exploitative, international, development
denounce	join, see, criticise, call for
consumer boycott	working conditions, management practice, press release, shopper protest

Task 2: which extracts describe problems and which extracts describe solutions? Underline the problem-signalling words.

Task 3: give the problem a name by creating a key concept for it.

Compare your answers with those suggested in the Answer section.

Comment ....

Extracts A to D describe a problem–solution cycle. At the end, the problem seems to return with *renewed criticism from development campaigners*. In the case study assignment, students are asked to solve this problem. An important step in solving any problem is to name it. As you will see, the assignment question does this.

5.3 Solutions: input text 2

As with all case study assignments, the assignment title is one of the input texts.

Activity 5.2 ....

Purpose: to identify the instruction word and key concepts in the assignment title.

Task 1: underline the key concepts in the following assignment title and circle the instruction words.

Assignment title

Gap takes great care with its vendor selection process but it continues to attract criticism for working conditions in some of its suppliers. Outline the key aspects of a vendor selection and monitoring process that will further Gap's long-term best interests.

Task 2: complete the following sentence with the most appropriate noun group.

Gap has a problem with _____

Task 3: which words in the second sentence make it clear that the action recommended in this assignment will improve the situation for Gap?

Compare your answers with those suggested in the Answer section.

Comment

As you saw in Session 4, it may be difficult to identify exactly what the problem is in a situation. Here, the problem-signalling word is *criticism* and the problem is *working conditions in some of its suppliers*. This was already obvious from Extract D in Activity 5.1. However, *working conditions* are actually the result of a different problem according to the question – something is wrong with *the vendor selection process*. This is a good example of how a particular concept can frame an analysis. In order to solve this problem, a student needs to have their own mind map of ideas around the concept, *vendor selection process*.

5.4 Proposing a solution: a student text

Extract E is the introduction to an assignment written by a student called Miriam who has such a mind map. Starting with the concept which is identified in the assignment question, Miriam introduces a new concept which forms the basis for her assignment.

Activity 5.3

Purpose: to notice how an introduction frames an analysis as a solution.

Task: quickly read through the introduction to the student assignment in Extract E. Then read it again and do the following tasks. Before doing this task, you may find it helpful to read a simplified version of this extract in the appendix to Resource Book 1 (Extract 5.1).

1   Mark where **the situation**, **the problem** and **the solution** in Extract E begin and end.

2   Which signal word tells you where the problem step begins?

3   Which words tell you where the solution step begins?

4   Which key concept does Miriam use to frame the solution?

Extract E

Gap continues to attract criticism for working conditions in some of its suppliers. Outline the key aspects of a vendor selection and monitoring process that will further Gap's long-term best interests.

Gap's current vendor selection policy focuses on a vendor's ability to meet product quality standards and production capacity at the right cost and also on whether they conform to ethical trading standards in line with the Code of Vendor Conduct.

However, this policy has not stopped criticism of the working practices of some of Gap's suppliers. It may therefore be beneficial for Gap to consider recent trends in vendor selection whereby organisations seek close long-term relationships with suppliers. These relationships are called 'partnership sourcing' and are considered mutually beneficial to both parties.

(Source: adapted from OUBS student assignment)

Compare your answers with those suggested in the Answer section.

Activity 5.4 ....

Purpose: to focus on the problem–solution pattern in Extract E.

Task: Extract E has been divided into its different steps below. Write the following labels next to the appropriate part of the text.

> solution (with suggestion words)
> justification for suggested solution
> situation
> name for solution
> problem (with problem-signalling words)

Gap's **current** vendor selection policy focuses on a vendor's ability to meet product quality standards and production capacity at the right cost and also on whether they conform to ethical trading standards in line with the Code of Vendor Conduct.	
However, this policy has not stopped **criticism** of the working practices of some of Gap's suppliers.	
It may therefore be beneficial for Gap to consider recent trends in vendor selection whereby organisations seek close long-term relationships with suppliers.	
These relationships are called '**partnership sourcing**'	
and **are considered** mutually beneficial to both parties.	

Compare your answers with those suggested in the Answer section.

Comment ....

Like many well-written texts, this assignment starts at a high level of generalisation. The introduction relates directly to the question it is answering. It names the key concepts it will use to frame the case and, because it is a text proposing a solution, it uses the problem–solution pattern as a way of organising the introduction.

Miriam has a mind map of ideas around the concept of *vendor selection* which means that she can propose solutions to the problem. But where does this mind map come from? How can you find solutions? As with all output texts, they come from input texts. The guidance notes accompanying the assignment title explain this as follows.

An obvious source for this part would be the Module 3 discussion on Toyota. It would also be worth reading Chapter 11 of the Reader on supply chain management.

In the next activity you will read an extract from the text which Miriam read to develop her mind map about partnership sourcing.

5.5 Solutions: input text 3

One place to find solutions is in other cases where solutions to similar problems have been tried. The Toyota text referred to in the guidance notes is one of these cases. It is a *Financial Times* story about Toyota's vendor selection process. You will read an extract from this article as background to the student's assignment on partnership sourcing. Before doing this task, you may find it helpful to read a simplified version of the extract in the appendix to Resource Book 1 (Extract 5.3).

Activity 5.5 ....

Purpose: to introduce the Toyota text and a key concept for the assignment.

Task 1: quickly look through Extract 5.2 to get a general idea of what it is about.

Task 2: now read Extract 5.2 more carefully. As you read each paragraph, choose a sentence from the list below which summarises it best.

Paragraph 1
1   Partnership sourcing is a kind of relationship marketing.
2   Partnership sourcing is a kind of supplier selection.
3   Purchasing is carried out by suppliers.

Paragraph 2
The article shows how Toyota:
1   produces car parts
2   purchases car parts
3   supplies car parts.

Paragraph 3
Toyota is selecting:
1   companies that would like to become car-part producers
2   companies that would like to produce cars
3   companies that would like to supply car-parts to Toyota.

Paragraph 4
1   Toyota controls suppliers.
2   Toyota depends on suppliers.
3   Toyota has problems with suppliers.

Paragraph 5
1   Toyota uses mostly Japanese suppliers.
2   Toyota uses mostly European suppliers.
3   About half of Toyota's suppliers are European.

Paragraph 6

1   Toyota says it is using local suppliers.
2   Toyota is paying a lot for local suppliers.
3   Toyota is using local suppliers.

Paragraph 7

1   Toyota does not set up Japanese transplants.
2   Toyota has set up a few Japanese transplants.
3   Transplants and prototypes are the same.

Paragraph 8

1   Toyota expects long-term partnerships with 2000 companies.
2   Toyota wants long-term partnerships.
3   The list has 2000 companies.

Compare your answers with those suggested in the Answer section.

Comment   ....

The extracts you have read in Activities 5.1 to 5.5 provide the background to the solution text you will read next. In Sessions 1 to 4 you focused on the situation in the case study text itself. Although you framed your analysis with business concepts from outside the case, you analysed what was happening in the case.

When you write a solution text, you are looking at a situation which is not in the case study. You are proposing something new. As you have seen, this involves using input texts such as the Toyota one. In the next section you will look more closely at how to use input texts like this creatively.

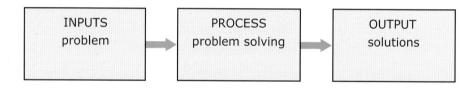

5.6 Proposing solutions: an output text

Activity 5.6   ....

Purpose: to get an overview of a student text that proposes a solution.

Task: Extract F is the first four paragraphs of Miriam's text on Gap's vendor selection process. You have already seen the first two paragraphs. In the right-hand column there are three sets of concept notes for each paragraph. Tick the notes that best summarise each paragraph. The first one is done for you as an example.

Before doing this task, you may find it helpful to read a simplified version of this text in the appendix to Resource Book 1 (Extract 5.5).

Extract F

Student text	Summary
Gap continues to attract criticism for working conditions in some of its suppliers. Outline the key aspects of a vendor selection and monitoring process that will further Gap's long-term best interests.	Tick the best summary for the paragraph
[Paragraph 1] Gap's current vendor selection policy focuses on a vendor's ability to meet product quality standards and production capacity at the right cost and also on whether they conform to ethical trading standards in line with the Code of Vendor Conduct.	**Paragraph 1** (a) Code of Vendor Conduct (b) Current vendor selection policy ✓ (c) Traditional purchasing policy
[Paragraph 2] However, this policy has not stopped criticism of the working practices of some of Gap's suppliers. It may therefore be beneficial for Gap to consider recent trends in vendor selection whereby organisations seek close long-term relationships with suppliers. These relationships are called 'partnership sourcing' and are considered mutually beneficial to both parties.	**Paragraph 2** (a) Continuing criticism and recent trends in vendor selection (b) Working practices and mutual benefit (c) Continuing criticism and partnership sourcing
[Paragraph 3] If Gap was interested in partnership sourcing it would have to significantly reduce the number of vendors it deals with. As Bryan Jackson, director of Toyota Motor Manufacturing UK points out 'It's rather difficult to have a relationship with 1,000 suppliers ... It's much better to have fewer, who are more closely involved' (OU-B200, Study Guide 3, p. 38).	**Paragraph 3** (a) Reduction in number of vendors (b) Toyota's methods (c) Thousands of suppliers
[Paragraph 4] Vendors could be selected to provide a larger share of the organisation's business, supplying whole product groups (one vendor for jeans; one for T-shirts, etc.). What Gap should be looking for in these suppliers is more than just their ability to deliver the product. It should also look for an understanding of company philosophy, management capability and attitude, and development capability. These are the items which the Toyota selection system, for example, pays significant attention to.	**Paragraph 4** (a) Company philosophy (b) Management capability (c) Whole product groups and characteristics of vendors

(Source: OUBS student assignment)

Compare your answers with those suggested in the Answer section.

Comment ....

As with all the tasks in this course which focus on key concepts, these concepts give an overview of the text. They stay at a high level and leave out the details. However, these lower-level details are important for proposing solutions. They are not *unnecessary* details.

Levels in a solution text

Activity 5.7 ....

Purpose: to demonstrate the relationship between high-level concepts and low-level details in a student assignment.

Task: in the version of Extract F below the high-level concepts are in bold and the lower level details are underlined. Why are the lower-level details necessary?

Extract F (with levels highlighted)

> **Gap continues to attract criticism for working conditions in some of its suppliers. Outline the key aspects of a vendor selection and monitoring process that will further Gap's long-term best interests.**
>
> *[Paragraph 1]*
>
> Gap's **current vendor selection policy** focuses on a vendor's ability to meet product quality standards and production capacity at the right cost and also on whether they conform to ethical trading standards in line with the Code of Vendor Conduct.
>
> *[Paragraph 2]*
>
> However, this policy has not stopped **criticism** of the working practices of some of Gap's suppliers. It may therefore be beneficial for Gap to consider recent trends in vendor selection whereby organisations seek close long-term relationships with suppliers. These relationships are called '**partnership sourcing**' and are considered mutually beneficial to both parties.
>
> *[Paragraph 3]*
>
> If Gap was interested in partnership sourcing it would have to significantly **reduce the number of vendors** it deals with. As Bryan Jackson, director of Toyota Motor Manufacturing UK points out 'It's rather difficult to have a relationship with 1,000 suppliers ... It's much better to have fewer, who are more closely involved' (OU-B200, Study Guide 3, p. 38).
>
> *[Paragraph 4]*
>
> Vendors could be selected to provide a larger share of the organisation's business, supplying **whole product groups** (one vendor for jeans; one for T-shirts, etc.). **What Gap should be looking for in these suppliers** is more than just their ability to deliver the product. It should also look for an understanding of company philosophy, management capability and attitude, and development capability. These are the items which the Toyota selection system, for example, pays significant attention to.
>
> (Source: OUBS student assignmrnt)

The answers are discussed below.

Comment

This activity demonstrates how the key concepts organise the details of this solution text into paragraphs.

Each paragraph refers back to the concepts in the assignment title. Paragraph 1 refers back to the words *vendor selection and monitoring process.* Paragraph 2 refers back to *criticism* and a new *vendor selection and monitoring process that will further Gap's long-term best interests.* Paragraphs 3 and 4 begin the process of outlining *the key aspects of a vendor selection and monitoring process.* In this way, the key concepts of each paragraph keep the case study focused on the assignment title.

The details underlined in each paragraph develop the concepts. In paragraphs 3 and 4, the first sentence tells you what *key aspect* the paragraph will deal with. Then the remaining sentences in the paragraph move down to lower levels of detail or give examples to explain the key aspect.

5.7 Proposing solutions: the language

Generally, the solutions in a case study have already been tried and are in the past. The solutions in a student analysis have not yet been tried. They are for the future.

Activity 5.8

Purpose: to look more closely at the language for proposing solutions.

Task: below six solutions are listed. Three are **reported** solutions and were used in the past. Three are **proposed** solutions and could be used in the future.

1   Write **R** next to the **reported** solutions from the past and **P** next to the **proposed** solutions for the future.

2   Underline the language that told you which was which.

3   Look back at Extract F. Find two more examples of proposed solutions.

Solutions

(a) Vendors could be selected to provide a larger share of the organisation's business, supplying whole product groups (one vendor for jeans; one for T-shirts, etc.).

(b) The framework for Gap's corporate ethical values is set out in a Code of Vendor Conduct which Gap first produced in the early 1990s in response to criticisms of 'sweat shop' labour conditions among some of its vendors.

(c) If Gap was interested in partnership sourcing, it would have to significantly reduce the number of vendors it deals with.

(d) An American reporter stumbled upon a factory in Saipan, in the Pacific, where Gap clothes were being produced by a subcontractor who, unknown to Gap, was hiring Chinese labourers for 80-hour weeks at less than $2 an hour. The company quickly denounced and sacked the contractor.

(e) It may therefore be beneficial for Gap to consider recent trends in vendor selection whereby organisations seek close long-term relationships with suppliers.

(f) The report that Gap was hiring Chinese labourers for $2 an hour was unwelcome publicity for an organisation with native grasses planted on the roof of its San Francisco headquarters for eco-friendly insulation, and baby-friendly quiet rooms for nursing mothers (*The Guardian*, 23/11/01). As a result Gap Inc. produced the Code as a means of influencing working conditions and management practices in their vendor organizations.

Compare your answers with those suggested in the Answer section.

Comment

Often a solution from a different situation can be applied to the problem you are attempting to solve. However, to do this you need to change the language of reported solutions into the language of proposed solutions.

In Miriam's text, the main solution is:

> It may therefore be beneficial for Gap to consider recent trends in vendor selection whereby organisations seek close long-term relationships with suppliers. These relationships are called 'partnership sourcing'.

This solution was reported in the introduction to the Toyota case study as:

> Recent trends in purchasing have seen many organisations seeking to have much closer, long-term relationships with many fewer suppliers. The term 'partnership sourcing' has come into currency.

In other words, Miriam transfers the Toyota partnership sourcing solution to the Gap situation.

5.8 Solutions: input text 4

Paragraphs 3 and 4 of Miriam's assignment describe three aspects of the partnership sourcing solution. You will now read the part of the Toyota case study where they came from.

Activity 5.9 ....

Purpose: to read another extract of the Toyota case study and find the solutions proposed in the Gap analysis.

Task 1: Extract 5.6 in Resource Book 1 is the next part of the Toyota case study. It explains the *vendor selection process.*

Read the extract quickly to get an idea of what it is about. Then read it again more carefully and do the following task.

Before doing this task, you may find it helpful to read a simplified version of the extract in the appendix to Resource Book 1 (Extract 5.7).

Each of the six shortened sentences below summarises a step in the Toyota *vendor selection process*. The sentences are mixed up. Number the steps so they are in the same order as in the Toyota case study.

Summary sentences

(a) Award contracts for sample components.

(b) Evaluate abilities of vendors by judging important characteristics.

(c) Increase level of interaction.

(d) Reduce number to one-fifth of the original number.

(e) Gather information on all possible vendors.

(f) Cut number by almost half.

Task 2: in her assignment, Miriam proposes the following three aspects of the vendor selection process.

(i) Reduce the number of vendors.

(ii) Select vendors to provide a larger share of the organisation's business, supplying whole product groups (one vendor for jeans; one for T-shirts, etc.).

(iii) Look for an understanding of company philosophy, management capability and attitude, and development capability.

Look through Extract 5.6 and underline the sentences where Miriam found these ideas.

Compare your answers with those suggested in the Answer section.

Comment ....

All of the solutions Miriam proposes for Gap's problems come from the Toyota case study. Her skill is the creativity with which she transfers the solutions from Toyota to Gap.

5.9 Turning reported solutions into proposals

Once Miriam found the ideas for a solution *reported* in the case study, she had to turn them into *proposals* for the assignment. The difference between reported solutions and proposed solutions is in the **verbs.**

In the Toyota case study, the verbs refer to past or present time. For example:

- It **began** with Toyota compiling
- Toyota **assessed** capabilities
- The weeding out **reduced** the 400 to 250
- The first orders **were issued**
- This **means** an intensification of contacts

In Miriam's assignment, the verbs deal with future or imagined time. For example:

- It **may be** beneficial
- If Gap **was** interested **it would have to reduce**
- Vendors **could be selected**
- Gap **should be looking for**
- It **should also look for**

Here is a range of language for proposing solutions.

- If they want ... they should/could ...
- If they wanted to ... they would have to/this would require ...
- It might/may/could be beneficial/better/effective/profitable, etc.
- They should/could/ought to/must ...
- It is essential that they ...
- They may find it advisable to ...
- ... needs to be agreed/introduced/set up
- ... could have benefits

The sentences in the next activity originate from the third and final part of the Toyota case study. You do not have to read the full version of this extract. However, if you are interested, it is Extract 5.8 in Resource Book 1. There is no simplified version.

Activity 5.10

Purpose: to practise turning reported solutions into proposed solutions.

Task: the sentences below report on some more aspects of Toyota's vendor selection process. Use some of the proposal language listed above and change these reported solutions into proposed solutions for Gap. If possible, reduce the proposed solution by leaving out details or by generalising.

1 Toyota has given many presentations to all of the suppliers to inform them of its standards. Suppliers have been left in no doubt what those standards are. They constantly receive many detailed notes from meetings saying what has been discussed and understood between supplier and vehicle maker.

2 Toyota does not try to impose Japanese methods on suppliers. Japanese and European manufacturers have different ways of making some components. It is not cost-effective for a European factory to change its methods and lose all the money invested in that method. The European supplier can make the components in their own way as long as the product meets Toyota's standards.

3   There is a widespread belief that Japanese vehicle companies form business partnerships for life with suppliers. This is not true. Toyota's needs will change and business partnerships have to change as a result.

4   The 1850 suppliers who have not been chosen are treated with great respect. They may be selected sometime in the future when Toyota's needs change.

5   Toyota emphasises the need for partnership with suppliers rather than conflict. To achieve that, Toyota has set up technology 'help' teams. If a supplier does not really understand what Toyota wants, or how to go about it, these help teams go out and explain Toyota's production systems to them. The idea is to give assistance rather than check on what's been done.

Compare your answers with those suggested in the Answer section.

Comment

When you transfer a solution from one case study to another, you have to adapt the solution creatively. This is about being creative not only with ideas but also with language. How did Miriam do this?

Activity 5.11

Purpose: to see how a student text turns reported solutions into proposed solutions.

Task: Extract G is the next three paragraphs of Miriam's assignment. You can see the full version in Resource Book 1 (Text 5.4). Before doing this task, you may find it helpful to read a simplified version in the appendix to Resource Book 1 (Extract 5.5).

1   Underline the proposed solutions in Extract G.

2   Miriam found these solutions in the sentences you read in Activity 5.10. Compare what she has written here in Extract G with the sentences you wrote in Activity 5.10.

Extract G

[Paragraph 5]

This form of customer-supplier relationship is obviously different to that previously experienced by Gap's vendors. Therefore it is essential that Gap make their new standards and requirements clear, especially to vendors who have previously supplied Gap. The objectives of the relationship need to be agreed between the two parties. Gap may find it advisable to award prototype contracts to give vendors a feel for what it is like working with Gap in this new way.

[Paragraph 6]

Once selected any subsequent monitoring system of vendors should be used to reinforce not weaken the relationship and so should not just be a tool for criticism but also one that recognises improvement. It should be based on key agreed performance measures and used to provide feedback, encourage improvement and reinforce Gap's expectations. Any vendor struggling to achieve its targets should be encouraged to work with Gap through, for example, a vendor development or improvement group.

[Paragraph 7]

The information provided by the monitoring system must also be sufficient to enable decisions on sourcing for future products to be made. Although Gap and its vendors should develop joint long-term business strategies, they must recognise business partnerships are not necessarily for life. Environmental changes may mean that a previously rejected vendor becomes more suitable to the organisation's needs. Gap could also change what they require from their suppliers, for example they may look for companies who can design, develop and produce products and this would require vendors with different capabilities to those just selected for production.

Compare your answers with those suggested in the Answer section.

Comment

Miriam changes

Toyota has set up technology 'help' teams

to

Any vendor struggling to achieve its targets should be encouraged to work with Gap through a vendor development or improvement group.

To do this, first she develops the original Toyota idea and adapts it to the Gap situation. Second, she turns a past tense verb – *has set up* – into a different kind of verb – *should be encouraged*. These kinds of verbs are called **modal verbs**. They are the language for proposing solutions.

5.10 Organising solution texts

You have already seen that Miriam uses *aspects of the vendor selection process* to organise her ideas in paragraphs 3 and 4.

Paragraph 3	Reduction in number of vendors
Paragraph 4	Vendors who provide whole product groups and characteristics of vendors

She continues this in paragraphs 5 to 7.

Activity 5.12 ···

Purpose: to notice the organisation of paragraphs 5 to 7 of Miriam's assignment.

Task: look at Extract G in Activity 5.11. Match each of the following concepts to one of the paragraphs.

changing nature of relationship over time

monitoring – a tool for improvement

need for clarity on new standards

Compare your answers with those suggested in the Answer section.

Comment ···

Once again, the key concepts that you have just matched to paragraphs 5–7 are abstract nouns but a solution needs to include **actions**. In the next activity you will look at how Miriam uses these abstract nouns to organise the actions that she proposes.

Activity 5.13 ···

Purpose: to notice how high-level concepts organise groups of actions in a paragraph.

Task 1: paragraphs 5 to 7 below propose a key concept of partnership sourcing. Identify the actions that make up each aspect. Paragraph 5 is done for you as an example.

Paragraph 5

Key concept	*Need for clarity on new standards*
Actions	Make new standards and requirements clear
	Agree objectives of relationship
	Award prototype contracts

Paragraph 6

Key concept _____

Actions _____

_____

_____

Paragraph 7

Key concept _____

Actions _____

_____

_____

Compare your answers with those suggested in the Answer section.

5.11 Justifying a proposed solution

At the beginning of this session a solution was said to be like an answer to a question. In fact, a solution text is an answer to three questions:

- What is the problem?
- What is your solution?
- Why do you think so?

An important part of a solution is the justification for it.

Miriam answers the second question in paragraph 2.

- What is your solution?

> It may therefore be beneficial for Gap to consider recent trends in vendor selection whereby organisations seek close long-term relationships with suppliers. These relationships are called 'partnership sourcing'.

She gives the justification in the last words of the paragraph.

- Why do you think so?

> are considered mutually beneficial to both parties.

This justification refers to the benefits. Eight ways of justifying a proposed solution are listed below. Most of these are used somewhere in Miriam's text.

1   Refer to another business where the solution was successful.

> This approach has proved profitable in Asda.

2   Explain that a desired outcome depends on the proposed action.

> If Wal-Mart want to be successful in the UK, they will have to recognise that supermarkets in the UK are different to those in the US.

3   Explain that the proposal is logical (using signal words like *so* and *therefore*).

> The government has changed its policy on out of town shopping centres, so Asda should find a way to move into the town centres.

4   Explain that the proposal is logical (by organising the sentences
     to show this, but not using signal words).

> The company is slipping into bankruptcy. It should ask its share-
> holders for more money.

5   Explain what the purpose of the proposed action is.

> The company should take out a loan to help it through the immediate
> problems.

6   Describe the benefits of the proposed solution.

> The introduction of a loyalty card would increase the number of
> customers.

7   Compare the proposed solution with a different course of
     action.

> Gap might be able to avoid major controversy with its current vendor
> selection system but negative publicity is much less likely with a part-
> nership sourcing process.

8   Quote an authority figure.

> As Bryan Jackson, director of Toyota Motor Manufacturing UK, points
> out 'It's rather difficult to have a relationship with 1,000 suppliers'.

Activity 5.14

Purpose: to see how the proposed solutions in Miriam's assignment are justified.

Task: look at paragraphs 3 to 7 of Text 5.4. How does Miriam justify her proposed solutions?

Compare your answers with those suggested in the Answer section.

Comment

Miriam uses several justifications to show that the solutions from Toyota's situation are relevant to Gap's situation.

5.12 Solutions: the conclusion

In her concluding paragraph, Miriam demonstrates how her assignment has answered the assignment question. She brings together all the key aspects of partnership sourcing and shows how it is *beneficial to both parties*.

Activity 5.15

Purpose: to notice how the final paragraph justifies the solution by pointing out its benefits.

Task: the assignment title and the final paragraph are given below again.

1   Identify any words in the final paragraph which refer back to the **title** of the assignment.

2   Identify any words in the first sentence of the paragraph which signal that this paragraph will provide a **justification** for the proposed solution.

3   Which of the following noun groups is the best summary of the main **benefit** of the solution?

closer relationships   fully integrated supply chain
reduction of late deliveries

> **Outline the key aspects of a vendor selection and monitoring process that will further Gap's long-term best interests.**
>
> *[Paragraph 8]*
>
> Developing closer relationships with its suppliers could have significant benefits for Gap in securing its long-term future. The closer relationship with their supply base could be used strategically by Gap, with the management team managing the whole process from vendor to customer as a fully integrated supply chain. This would help Gap monitor their vendor's working conditions more effectively and give the vendors more support in meeting Gap's standards. There are likely to be many other benefits from partnership sourcing. For example, it could help to reduce the late deliveries and inventory problems that Gap experienced in 2000.

Compare your answers with those suggested in the Answer section.

Comment ....

The final paragraph makes clear the benefits of the solution. This is the most important purpose of a solution-oriented assignment.

The paragraph also introduces a new key concept into the text – *fully integrated supply chain*. Here, Miriam is responding to this advice in the assignment notes:

> **It would also be worth reading Chapter 11 of the Reader on supply chain management.**

Supply chain management is an important key concept in the business studies course Miriam is studying. You may also have noticed it in the Gap case study you read at the end of Session 4 (Text 4.5). The final activity based on Miriam's assignment is to read the text where she found this concept.

Activity 5.16 ....

Purpose: to examine why the concept of *a fully integrated supply chain* is relevant to Gap's vendor selection problems.

Task 1: read Extract 5.9 'The supply chain and competitive performance' in Resource Book 1 and write three or four sentences to explain the concept of *a fully integrated supply chain*.

Task 2: does the text refer to the kind of vendor problems that Gap experienced?

Task 3: write a few more sentences to explain the connection between *a fully integrated supply chain* and Gap's vendor problems.

Compare your answers with those in the Answer section.

Comment

Supply chain management could be a major concept in the solution to Gap's problems. It is probably not a good idea to introduce such a big idea in the conclusion of the analysis. There is not time to develop it and provide justifications for proposing it. However, it is a good example of how a key business studies concept can be used to frame a solution in an analysis.

5.13 Comparing solution texts

In this section, you will look at two other assignments on the vendor selection process written by different students. The assignment title is the same as the one you have examined in this session. So, in some ways, these texts are similar to the one you have already looked at; but, in other ways, they are different. The reason for this activity is that it is important to notice that good assignments are not all written in the same way.

Optional Activity 5.17

Purpose: to revise what makes a solution assignment successful and to recognise different ways of achieving this success.

Task: Texts 5.10 and 5.11 in Resource Book 1 are solution assignments. Use the Reflection pages at the end of this session to help you compare Texts 5.10 and 5.11 with Miriam's assignment, which you have been studying in this session. Write your reflections in your Learning Journal.

Comment

There is no answer or comment on this activity.

5.14 Writing a solution text

Activity 5.18

Purpose: to write a solution text, using the knowledge and skills introduced in this session.

Task: Text 5.12 in Resource Book 1 is an extract from a case study of Nike. It deals with a similar problem to Gap's *vendor selection and monitoring process*. However, the solution that Nike uses is different from Gap's. The solution is in the last part of the text.

Read Text 5.12 and then write a new solution text for the problems at Gap. Instead of using the concepts of *partnership sourcing* and *supply chain management* to frame the solution, use the concept of *corporate responsibility* as explained in Text 5.12.

Comment

5.15 Vocabulary activity

See the course website for how to do a vocabulary-building activity for this session.

5.16 Critical reflection

The Reflection section below outlines the skills and knowledge you have practised during this session. In your Learning Journal, spend about 30 minutes reflecting on the learning outcomes of this session, using the Reflection pages as a guide. How far have you achieved these outcomes?

Reflection

Situation: Proposing solutions

Figure 5.1   The solution writing process

Communication skills

Producing output texts that propose solutions

1   Read the case study to identify the problems in the case.
2   If possible, give the problems business-concept names.
3   Search for solutions from course books.
4   If possible, give the solutions business-concept names
5   Transfer the solutions to the case study.
6   Produce a text that responds to the assignment title, instructions and concepts.
7   Produce introduction paragraphs that connect with the title, the problem and the solution.
8   Produce more paragraphs with high-level generalisations and concepts and low-level details, examples and actions.
9   Suggest solutions using proposing language.
10   Provide a justification for the solutions.
11   Produce a conclusion that refers back to the title and introduction, points out the benefits of the proposed solution and the added value in the assignment.

Language knowledge

How solution texts are organised

- Introduction refers to the assignment title and establishes the problem.
- Then it identifies the solution at a high level of generalisation.
- The solution may be named using concept words.
- The text then moves through aspects of the solution.
- Levels in text:
    high level – generalisations and key concepts
    low level – examples, details, actions
- Conclusion generalises the benefits of the solution, refers back to the title and makes clear the added value of the assignment.

How texts are structured

- Beginning paragraphs set the scene for the text.
- Beginning sentences of paragraphs set the general situation of paragraph.

How sentences are structured

- Nouns and verbs
- Proposal verbs

How word groups are structured

- Noun groups
- Verb groups

Business studies knowledge

- Supply chain management
- Supplier selection and monitoring
- Partnership sourcing
- Vendor compliance management

5.17 Answer section

Activity 5.1

Task 1

Extract A

The true statements are:

2   The companies that make Gap clothes are called vendors.

4   The Code of Vendor Conduct deals with ethical standards among vendors.

Vocabulary
sourcing = obtaining; **vendor** = supplier; **ethical values** = code of conduct; **vetting** = inspecting

Extract B

The true statement is:

1   The factory in Saipan was an example of a 'sweat shop'.

Vocabulary
subcontractor = supplier; **working conditions** = rate of pay

Extract C

The true statement is:

4   If the vendor does not improve, the Vendor Compliance Officers terminate business with the vendor.

Vocabulary
to comply with = to abide by; **commitments** = agreements; **breaches of the code** = breaking of the code.

Extract D

There are no true statements.

Vocabulary
abusive = exploitative; **denounce** = criticise; **consumer boycott** = shopper protest.

Task 2

Extract A is a positive solution-oriented paragraph. Positive words include: *rigorous processes of prior vetting and monitoring against company standards*; *ensuring that a manufacturer meets the required quality standards and has the capacity to accept a particular order*; *in response to criticisms*.

Extract B is a negative problem-oriented paragraph. Negative words include: *shine was first tarnished*; *stumbled upon a factory*; *denounced and sacked*; *unwelcome publicity*.

Extract C is solution-oriented. Positive words include: *Their objective is to ensure Gap Inc.'s vendor organizations understand the company's ethical commitments and that they abide by them as closely as possible allowing for differences in cultural context*; *Gap's approach is to encourage continuous improvement but where serious breaches of the Code of Conduct or a pattern of non-compliance occur, they suspend or terminate business with the vendor.*

Extract D is problem-oriented. Negative words include: *the company came in for renewed criticism*; *to publicise and denounce what they saw as 'abusive working conditions'*; *campaigners called for a consumer boycott.*

Task 3

This is answered in the next activity.

Activity 5.2

Task 1

Assignment title

Gap takes great care with its <u>vendor selection process</u> but it continues to attract <u>criticism for working conditions in some of its suppliers.</u> Outline the key aspects <u>of a vendor selection and monitoring process</u> that will <u>further Gap's long-term best interests.</u>

Task 2

Gap has a problem with its vendor selection process.

Task 3

The answer is: *will further Gap's long-term best interests.*

Activity 5.3

The first paragraph of this assignment outlines the **situation** with the words *Gap's current vendor selection policy.* In the second paragraph, the words *however* and *criticism* signal that this is a **problem**. The **solution** is signalled by the positive word *beneficial.* It is also signalled by **suggestion language**: *It may therefore be beneficial.*

So the second paragraph is a problem–solution paragraph. The solution is *organisations seek close long-term relationships with suppliers.* Miriam uses a business concept to frame this solution: *partnership sourcing.* Finally, there is a justification for this solution: *These relationships ... are considered mutually beneficial to both parties.*

Activity 5.4

Gap's **current** vendor selection policy focuses on a vendor's ability to meet product quality standards and production capacity at the right cost and also on whether they conform to ethical trading standards in line with the Code of Vendor Conduct.	situation
However, this policy has not stopped **criticism** of the working practices of some of Gap's suppliers.	problem (with problem-signalling words)
It may therefore be beneficial for Gap to consider recent trends in vendor selection whereby organisations seek close long-term relationships with suppliers.	solution (with suggestion words)
These relationships are called **'partnership sourcing'**	name for solution
and **are considered** mutually beneficial to both parties.	justification for suggested solution

Activity 5.5

P1   2 Partnership sourcing is a kind of supplier selection

P2   The article shows how Toyota:
2 purchases car parts.

P3   Toyota is selecting:
3 companies that would like to supply car parts to Toyota.

P4   2 Toyota depends on suppliers.

P5   2 Toyota uses mostly European suppliers.

P6   3 Toyota is using local suppliers'

P7   1 Toyota does not set up Japanese transplants.

P8   2 Toyota wants long-term partnerships.

Activity 5.6

P1   (b) Current vendor selection policy

P2   (c) Continuing criticism and partnership sourcing

P3   (a) Reduction in number of vendors

P4   (d) Whole product groups and characteristics of vendors

Activity 5.8

Reported solutions

(b)   The framework for Gap's corporate ethical values is set out in a Code of Vendor Conduct which Gap <u>first produced</u> in the early 1990s <u>in response</u> to criticisms of 'sweat shop' labour conditions among some of its vendors.

(d)   An American reporter stumbled upon a factory in Saipan, in the Pacific, where Gap clothes were being produced by a subcontractor who, unknown to Gap, was hiring Chinese labourers for 80-hour weeks at less than $2 an hour. The company <u>quickly denounced and sacked</u> the contractor.

(f)   The report that Gap was hiring Chinese labourers for $2 an hour was unwelcome publicity for an organisation with native grasses planted on the roof of its San Francisco headquarters for eco-friendly insulation, and baby-friendly quiet rooms for nursing mothers. (*The Guardian* 23/11/01). <u>As a result Gap Inc. produced</u> the Code as a means of influencing working conditions and management practices in their vendor organizations.

Proposed solutions

(a)   Vendors <u>could be selected</u> to provide a larger share of an organisation's business, supplying whole product groups (one vendor for jeans; one for T-shirts, etc.).

(c)   <u>If</u> Gap <u>was interested</u> in partnership sourcing <u>it would have to</u> significantly reduce the number of vendors it deals with.

(e)   It <u>may therefore be beneficial</u> for Gap to consider recent trends in vendor selection whereby organisations seek close long-term relationships with suppliers.

Two more solutions

1   What Gap <u>should be looking for</u> in these suppliers is more than just their ability to deliver the product.

2   It <u>should also look for</u> an understanding of company philosophy, management capability and attitude, and development capability.

Activity 5.9

Task 1

(e)   Gather information on all possible vendors.

(d)   Reduce number to one-fifth of the original number.

(b)   Evaluate abilities of vendors by judging important characteristics.

(f)   Cut number by almost half.

(a)   Award contracts for sample components.

(c)   Increase level of interaction.

Task 2

The sentences where Miriam found her ideas are:

(i)   'It's much better to have fewer, who are more closely involved.'

(ii)   Closer involvement in Toyota's case has meant short-listed companies being asked to quote for entire product groups, not individual components, 'to give them a larger, more worthwhile chunk of the business,' says Jackson.

(iii)   At the 400-candidate stage, the selection process became much more painstaking. Over a period of 10 months a number of multidisciplinary Toyota teams assessed capabilities according to four key criteria:

1   management capability and attitude;

2   production and manufacturing facilities, and level of investment in technology;

3   quality control systems and philosophy;

4   research and development capability.

Activity 5.10

1   It could be beneficial if Gap gave presentations to all of the suppliers to inform them of its standards. Suppliers should be left in no doubt what those standards are. It is essential that they receive notes from meetings saying what has been discussed.

2   Gap should not try to impose its culture on suppliers. It may not be advisable for suppliers to change their methods and lose all the money invested in that method. The supplier should be allowed to make the components in their own way as long as the production process meets Gap's ethical standards.

3   It is essential that suppliers should not think the business partnership is for life.

4   Gap may find it advisable to treat suppliers they do not select with great respect.

5   If Gap wants partnership with suppliers rather than conflict it should set up technology 'help' teams. It is essential that the suppliers think the idea is to give assistance rather than check on what has been done.

Activity 5.11

1   The proposed solutions in Extract G are as follows.

Paragraph 5

... it is essential that Gap make their new standards and requirements clear ...

The objectives of the relationship need to be agreed between the two parties.

Gap may find it advisable to award prototype contracts to give vendors a feel for what it is like working with Gap in this new way.

Paragraph 6

... any subsequent monitoring system of vendors should be used to reinforce not weaken the relationship ...

... and so should not just be a tool for criticism ...

It should be based on key agreed performance measures ...

Any vendor struggling to achieve its targets should be encouraged to work with Gap through, for example, a vendor development or improvement group.

Paragraph 7

The information provided by the monitoring system must also be sufficient to enable decisions ...

Gap and its vendors should develop joint long-term business strategies ...

... they must recognise business partnerships are not necessarily for life.

... Gap could also change what they require from their suppliers ...

... for example they may look for companies who can ...

... this would require vendors with different capabilities to those just selected for production.

2   Did Miriam use the same proposal language as you did?

Activity 5.12

Paragraph 5	need for clarity on new standards
Paragraph 6	monitoring – a tool for improvement
Paragraph 7	changing nature of relationship over time

Activity 5.13

Paragraph 6

Key concept *monitoring, a tool for improvement*

Actions	Use subsequent monitoring of vendors to reinforce, not weaken, relationship
	Do not use as tool for criticism
	Use as tool to recognise improvement
	Base monitoring on key agreed performance measures
	Use to provide feedback, encourage improvement and reinforce expectations
	Encourage struggling companies to work with Gap through vendor development group

Paragraph 7

Key concept *changing nature of relationship over time*

Actions	Make sure information provided by the monitoring system is sufficient to decide on sourcing for future products.
	Develop joint long-term business strategies.
	Recognise business partnerships are not necessarily for life.
	Change what Gap require from their suppliers.
	Look for companies who can design, develop and produce products.

Activity 5.14

The number in brackets refers to the list of justifications.

Paragraph 3	logic (3) and referring to another business (1)
Paragraph 4	referring to another business (1)
Paragraph 5	logic (3) and purpose (5)
Paragraph 6	The second proposal is a logical result of the first proposal (3); but there is no justification for the first proposal.
Paragraph 7	logical result of *environmental changes* (3)

Activity 5.15

1 ... securing its long-term future.
2 ... could have significant benefits for Gap ...
3 fully integrated supply chain

Activity 5.16

Task 1

A company which has a fully integrated supply chain treats its suppliers as part of the total system that makes up its business. Instead of seeing suppliers as competitors who are seeking to make profit out of the company, a company with a fully integrated supply chain sees suppliers as partners. The closer the relationship between the suppliers and the company, the better it is for both parties.

Task 2

Yes.

Task 3

The reason why supply-chain integration could be an effective arrangement for Gap is that Gap is so dependent on its suppliers. Gap does not make any of its products. It has outsourced this to vendors. While Gap may have no responsibility for the physical work of producing its clothing, it cannot also give up responsibility for the conditions of the workers producing that clothing. It is as if these workers are Gap employees. In this situation, it makes more sense for Gap to take responsibility for their wellbeing by operating a fully integrated supply chain system.

SESSION **6 Evaluating the analysis**

6.1 Introduction

Through this book, we hope you have developed the skills of analysing business cases. Each session has focused on one of the skills needed to produce successful analyses. In this final session of Book 1, you will draw together the skills and knowledge you have studied in the last five sessions.

There are many kinds of case study in the world of business studies.

- Case studies can be about: a sector (private, public or voluntary); an industry (for example, the airline industry); an organisation (for example, Hope Hospital, the AA, Gap or Nike); or people (for example, the new head of sales).

- Case studies can be about different areas of business: organisational structure, environment and processes; human resources; finance; or marketing.

- Case analysis tasks can ask you to: summarise; describe; outline; explain; evaluate; compare and contrast; suggest; or recommend.

- Analyses can be framed by a wide range of business concepts, including: STEP; stakeholder; SWOT; external environment; vendor selection; market performance; or supply chain integration.

This is just a small sample of the concepts that can frame business case analysis.

By carrying out the instructions in the assignment task, using the processes you have practised in Sessions 1 to 5 and the business concepts from your business studies course, a case study is transformed into an analysis (Figure 6.1).

In this last session on evaluation, the focus is on how persuasive your output text is.

In a business system, the outputs are goods or services. If the business is going to succeed, these outputs have to appeal to consumers. The appeal of the product in the marketplace depends on

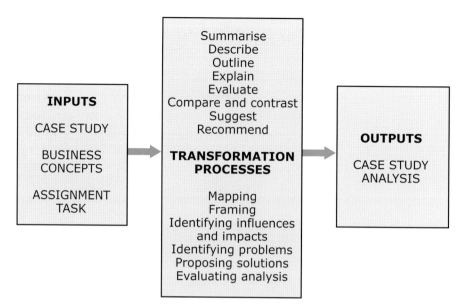

Figure 6.1 The process of writing a case study analysis

selecting the right inputs, processing them appropriately and presenting the product effectively. Market appeal cannot be added on at the end of the process.

It is the same for a business case analysis. The success of the analysis which you produce depends on the whole analysis process: which input texts you have processed, how effectively you have processed them, and how well designed your output text is. The success of your analysis will be obvious from the grade your tutor gives it. Your tutor is the consumer in this market. You have to persuade your tutor to 'buy' your product.

Under the heading of 'Evaluation', this session includes the skills of judgement, explanation, and persuasion. In fact, the five skills you have practised so far all involve judgement and explanation. If you have used these skills in your analysis, your output text will already be persuasive. However, it is possible to present your judgements and explanations more – or less – persuasively.

So this session focuses on the quality and appeal of your analysis. You will practise how to use text structure and the language of evaluation to judge, explain and persuade.

Learning outcomes

In this session you will develop the skills of:

- identifying your audience and purpose when writing your analysis; structuring the analysis according to the assignment instructions and concepts

- summarising as a form of evaluation

- recognising different points of view in case studies

- using data from the case study as evidence

- referencing case studies and business studies texts

- using the language of evaluation to judge, explain and persuade.

6.2 Persuasion in everyday life

Persuasion is all around you in your everyday life. Every time you listen to a commercial radio station, read a local newspaper, watch a television programme or read the advertisements on billboards, people are trying to persuade you to do something. Think of the companies which try to persuade you to buy their pizzas (Dominos, Pizza Hut, etc.), mobile phone services (Orange, T-Mobile, O2, etc.), television sets (Samsung, Sony, Philips, etc.) or personal computers (Dell, Packard Bell, etc.).

Activity 6.1

Purpose: to notice some features of persuasion in everyday life.

Task: in your daily life, you may come across mobile phone advertisements, which are one attempt at persuasion. Read one such advertisement below quickly. Which of these features would be important to you in choosing any of these mobile phones? Why?

Features:

- In-built MP3 player
- 900 any time, any network free minutes
- Half-price line rental
- A particular brand of handset such as Nokia and Samsung
- Colour of the handset
- Free Bluetooth set

An advertisement for mobile phones from the internet (to be used in Activity 6.1)

6.3 Evaluation in business studies

In order to be persuaded, your reader needs an analysis that is:

- based on evidence from the case study and other reading
- has been processed using appropriate concepts
- demonstrates the value of any proposed solutions
- is clearly organised.

The next activity shows how all these four factors involve evaluation.

Evaluation was introduced in Session 4 as part of the
problem–solution pattern. In a simple problem–solution text,
evaluation is most obvious at the end. In the sequence of questions in
Session 4, the evaluation question was the last one:

How successful is the solution?

In everyday life, this is what people want to know about solutions. In
a business case analysis, there is no real chance to evaluate the
solutions. They have not been tried in the real world. However, as you
will see in later activities, the end of an analysis is still a place where
much evaluation is done.

In fact, evaluation happens throughout the whole analysis process.
The next activity is based on the introductory paragraph of an
analysis written by a student.

Activity 6.2 ....

Purpose: to explore the role of evaluation in an analysis further.

Task: read Extract A below which is from the start of the assignment
on Gap's vendor selection processes which you read in Session 5.
Then answer the following questions.

1   What is the situation described?

2   What is the problem?

3   What is the solution proposed?

Extract A

> ### Gap takes great care with its vendor selection process but it continues to attract criticism for working conditions in some of its suppliers. Outline the key aspects of a vendor selection and monitoring process that will further Gap's long-term best interests.
>
> #### *Recognising the importance of the supply chain*
>
> In many respects, Gap's long-term success depends upon its supply chain. However, as the case study points out, Gap clothing was produced in three thousand factories in over fifty countries in 2002. For a multinational corporation such as Gap, the selection process is perhaps manageable but with so many factories to oversee, the monitoring process would require an army of Vendor compliance officers. Reducing the number of suppliers that the company uses might overcome this problem (see Toyota case study, Study Guide, Module 3) but a better way would be to try to integrate external suppliers into the Gap 'system'. This sounds paradoxical but essentially it is about Gap and its suppliers viewing the supply chain as a unitary system. Obviously, when one part of the system fails, it has adverse effects on other parts so it is in Gap's interest to integrate external vendors into its own system of production, distribution, standards and ethics. In this sense, the supply chain is not just about what Gap does but also about the way that it does it.
>
> (Source: OU Business School student assignment)

Compare your answers with those suggested in the Answer section.

Comment

In Extract A, the writer is trying to persuade the reader (her tutor) to accept her solutions by weighing up the situation, the existing problem, possible solutions and the explanation. In fact, you might have noticed that this student evaluates the starting situation differently from Miriam's assignment in Session 5. What this shows is that evaluation or judgement actually takes place from the beginning to the end. There is an **evaluation cycle**.

Now you will look at Extract A again, to see how the evaluation cycle works. First, look at Figure 6.2.

The first sentence of the analysis describes Gap's current situation; that is, the supply chain is critical for Gap. The writer then goes on to identify the problem by evaluating this situation. Although Gap as a multinational company may be able to manage the vendor selection process, the large number of suppliers would need many resources (that is, many vendor compliance officers). This is a problem. Next, the writer suggests a possible solution as adopted by Toyota (reduction in the number of suppliers). However, she does not consider this will be effective as a long-term solution. She uses the words *might overcome this problem* to predict the success, which means this solution may not help Gap to solve its problem fully. So, she proposes an alternative solution: integration of Gap's suppliers

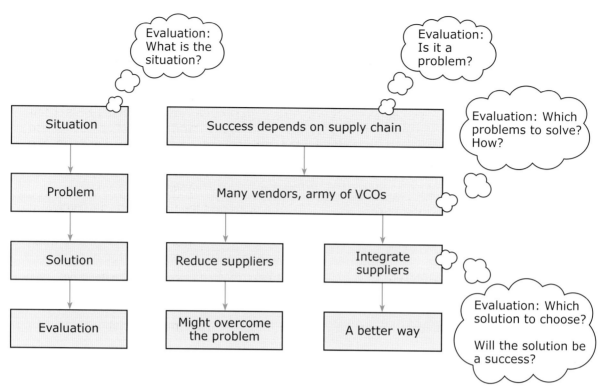

Figure 6.2 The evaluation cycle

into the Gap system. She then presents an explanation for this last solution which seems more convincing. This becomes the *unique selling point* of her analysis. It is different from the USP of the analysis you studied in Session 5. In Miriam's analysis, supply chain integration was not the main idea; it was introduced at the very end of the analysis. Figure 6.2 shows that evaluation occurs at every stage of the process.

The language of evaluation

As Activity 6.2 showed, evaluation is part of the structure of the text; but it also involves a certain kind of language. Evaluation language is language for judging, explaining and persuading. Here are some examples of evaluation language from Extract A.

> *In many respects, Gap's long-term success depends upon its supply chain.*
>
> *is perhaps manageable but ...would require an army*
>
> *might overcome this problem*
>
> *a better way would be to try to*
>
> *This sounds paradoxical but essentially it is about*
>
> *Obviously, when one part of the system fails, it has adverse effects on other parts so it is in Gap's interest to integrate external vendors into its own system of production, distribution, standards and ethics.*
>
> *In this sense, the supply chain is not just about what Gap does but also about the way that it does it*

The next activity looks at some of these words and their function in the extract.

Activity 6.3 ....

Purpose: to identify the link between the evaluation words and the problem- solution pattern.

Task: look at the words below, which are from Extract A. In the analysis each of them has a particular job to do. This is their function in the analysis. The right-hand column gives these functions but in the wrong order. Find each of the words in the extract and match them to one of the functions.

Words from Extract A	Function in the analysis
1 A better way	(a) It emphasises the value of the alternative solution.
2 Paradoxical	(b) It is an evaluation of an unsuccessful system and its relevance to Gap.
3 Essentially	(c) It describes and evaluates the negative meaning readers may attach to the alternative solution proposed.
4 Adverse effects	(d) It refers to an alternative solution and its evaluation.

Compare your answers with those suggested in the Answer section.

Comment ....

These words were used to evaluate the alternative solution and show how the writer understood the problem and its possible solution.

The success of your case study analysis depends on how effectively you use evaluative words like these to guide your reader through the analysis. Later in this session, there are more activities using this kind of evaluation language.

6.4 Carrying out the evaluation in a business case analysis

Case study assignments typically ask you to analyse the situation of the company in question. They may ask you to: summarise, describe, outline, explain, evaluate, compare and contrast, suggest or recommend. They may focus on areas such as the business environment, business structure, business processes, human resource management; finance; marketing, and so on. They may ask you to use business concepts or frameworks such as STEP, SWOT, five forces, organisational culture, relationship marketing, market segmentation, the four Ps, ratio analysis, motivation, hard or soft human resource management, and many more.

When writers write their analysis, they create certain patterns in their text. You have seen these patterns in previous sessions. Writers move up and down between high-level generalisations and lower-level details. They organise information according to business concepts. They sequence causes and effects. They identify problems, choose those which are important, find solutions and present the ones that are likely to be effective.

The purpose of these patterns is to explain the analysis and to persuade the reader to accept the analysis. In the next three activities you will look at the pattern of an analysis text.

Activity 6.4 ....

Purpose: to understand the assignment title.

Task: the analysis text you will study has the title:

Compare and contrast Gap's staff management with its outsourcing policy.

1   Underline the instruction words and the key concepts in the title.

2   For each key concept, choose the best definition from the four definitions below.

Definitions

The way a company obtains supplies.

The way a company treats its staff.

The way a company promotes staff.

The way a company contracts out some of its activity to other companies.

Compare your answers with those suggested in the Answer section.

Comment ....

This is a common type of assignment question in business studies. You must **compare** and **contrast** one aspect (*Gap's staff management*) with another (*its outsourcing policy*). When you compare things, the task is to explain how they are similar. When you contrast them, you explain how they are different. To do this, you must evaluate them.

You have seen the Gap case study in Sessions 3 to 5. In each session the analysis was framed by different concepts: stakeholder framework in Session 3; SWOT analysis in Session 4; and vendor selection processes and supply chain integration in Session 5. This time the two main concepts which will frame the analysis are *staff management policy* and *outsourcing policy*. Gap's outsourcing policy is already familiar from Session 5. (The case study is Text 3.2 in Resource Book 1). You were not asked to read the section on Gap's staff management policy carefully before. It is described in the section 'A good company to work for'. You might like to read that section of Text 3.2 before doing the next activity.

Stefan, who wrote the assignment below, used a range of business concepts from his business studies course. The first activity will focus your reading on those concepts.

Activity 6.5

Purpose: to understand Stefan's analysis.

Task: Text 6.1 in Resource Book 1 is Stefan's analysis. The notes in the right-hand column of the text are for the next activity so it is not necessary to read them yet. Look quickly through the analysis to get an idea of what it is about. Then read it more carefully and write answers to the questions below.

1 Why do Gap outsource their manufacturing and manage their staff in the way they do?

2 Find another noun group for the outsourcing Gap does.

3 For Gap, what is the benefit of the open market?

4 Name one effect of task specialisation.

5 What does Gap actually do?

6 'Which as I have already suggested is a peripheral process'. What words does Stefan use in the previous part of the analysis that suggest manufacturing is a 'peripheral process'?

7 Name one of the working conditions for core employees and one for peripheral employees.

8 Make a noun word group that names the environment in which Gap recruits its core staff.

9 How does this affect Gap's core staff management policy?

10 In the introduction the analysis says there is a single reason for both Gap's outsourcing and its management policy. Outsourcing reduces costs. What does 'corporate culture' do?

11 Give two reasons why Gap's corporate culture is not relevant to peripheral workers.

12 What concept connects Gap's staff management and outsourcing policies apart from 'optimal performance'?

13 An analysis is actually an argument. The analyst tries to persuade the reader that the points they are making are right. According to the conclusion, how many points are there in Stefan's analysis?

Compare your answers with those suggested in the Answer section.

Comment

Text 6.1 is Stefan's response to the assignment task. The instruction words and the key concepts in the title are fairly general. However, when Stefan sees the key concepts, *outsourcing* and *staff management*, he has an idea of what is expected of him. He has a mind map of information around these concepts. He knows the audience he is writing for and he knows the purpose of the writing.

Organisation of a compare-and-contrast analysis

The next activity focuses on the way Stefan has organised this analysis. The notes in the right-hand column of Text 6.1 describe how the analysis is organised.

Activity 6.6 ···

Purpose: to see how a compare and contrast analysis is organised.

Task: the notes in the right-hand column of Text 6.1 describe how the text is organised. These notes are not summaries of the content of the text. They describe how the text is organised. Five of these notes are inaccurate – they describe the text wrongly. Read each note in turn; compare it with the section of text it is next to. Find the five incorrect notes and correct them.

Compare your answers with those suggested in the Answer section.

Comment ···

To produce this analysis, Stefan used the skills of mapping, framing, identifying cause–effect and problems. As the last comment said, he uses the mind maps of knowledge he has developed on the business course. But, as he wrote the analysis, he used skills of evaluation – judging what to include, explaining what concepts mean and how one event leads to another, and persuading his reader to agree with him. One way in which he persuades his reader is by organising his text in a clear and logical pattern.

Text patterns

A text that compares two things can be organised in one of two ways.

Pattern 1: describe one feature of the first thing and compare this with a feature of the second thing. Then describe another feature of the first thing and compare it with a feature of the second thing.

Pattern 2: describe the first thing generally. Then describe the second thing generally. Then compare the features of both things.

Look at the two patterns in Figure 6.3. Which is Pattern 1 and which is Pattern 2?

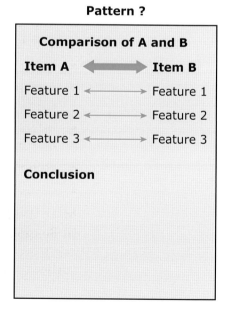

Figure 6.3 Types of text organisation in comparison texts

The pattern on the left is Pattern 2.

A text that compares and contrasts things can combine these two patterns in various ways. Figure 6.4 shows an example of a combined pattern – Pattern 3.

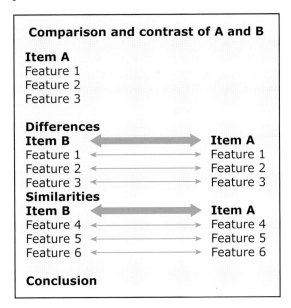

Figure 6.4 Type of text organisation in compare-and-contrast texts

Pattern 3 is closest to Stefan's assignment. In order to persuade his tutor to accept his analysis, he organised it in this way.

6.5 Evaluation in case analysis

As suggested earlier:

> evaluation = judgement + explanation + persuasion

The rest of this session will focus on how to judge, explain and persuade by:

- designing your analysis to fit with the assignment title and your audience's expectations (i.e. framing the case)
- summarising the case study input text (i.e. mapping the case)
- using the case study as evidence for your explanations
- noticing how different people in the case study have different ways of framing the case
- referencing the case study and the business studies course books
- recommending your analysis to your reader
- using persuasive language.

Most of this will be a revision of the skills you have already practised in Sessions 1 to 5. Only the skill of referencing the case study is completely new. However, the focus is now on the output text rather than the processing of the input text.

6.6 Designing analysis to fit the assignment title and audience expectations

In Sessions 1 to 5, you saw how analyses were designed in response to the instructions and key words of the assignment title. In this session, you have already seen how Stefan organised his text in a compare-and-contrast pattern in order to respond to the assignment title and communicate with his reader. The rest of this session looks at what else students do to meet tutors' expectations.

6.7 Summarising

Summarising was introduced in Session 1 where it was called *mapping the case*. It was pointed out that summarising involves three processes:

1   being clear about your motivation

2   selecting the information using levels in the text

3   reducing the information using key concepts.

All of these processes involve judgement. You have practised this kind of judgement many times in this book. The design of your output text – the analysis – depends on this judgement.

Activity 6.7 ....

Purpose: to compare the summaries in two output texts.

Task: Extracts B and C below are from two different assignments with the title 'Compare and contrast Gap's staff management with its outsourcing policy'. (Extract B is by Stefan and Extract C is by Santosh.) They both summarise the information in the Gap case study on *outsourcing*. The general motivation for each student was the same – to produce a successful assignment. This activity looks at the information they selected and how they reduced it.

1 Selection

(a) Extract C gives the advantages of outsourcing with four bullet points. Number each bullet point in Extract C (from 1 to 4). Then look for the same information in Extract B. Underline the information in Extract B and number it.

(b) Does Extract B contain the information for all the bullet points?

(c) Does Extract B contain any information not included in Extract C?

(d) Does Extract B contain the information from the first two sentences of Extract C? Where?

2 Reduction

(a) Sentence 3 in Extract C defines *outsourcing* using a clause. Underline the clause. Extract B defines outsourcing using an abstract noun group. Draw a box round this noun group.

(b) Extract C says that outsourcing gives Gap *a number of advantages*. What is the noun group used in Extract B for this idea? It contains more information and is a more specialised business concept.

(c) Each of the bullet points in Extract C is a shortened sentence. What noun groups does Extract B use for the second and fourth bullet points?

(d) One noun group in Extract B gives an advantage which is not included in Extract C. What is it?

(e) Extract B also uses a different noun group for outsourcing which is not used in Extract C. What is it?

Extract B – Stefan	Extract C – Santosh
Outsourcing [1]In Gap's case, outsourcing refers to the externalisation of its production processes. [2]Gap chooses the open market for the manufacturing of its garments as opposed to producing them internally because of the benefits that the open market provides. [3]Labour markets in foreign countries provide cheaper sources of the routine labour required in the manufacturing process than Gap can find in its home markets. [4]Effective management of the supply chain can lead to competitive advantage through cost reduction, (labour and materials), output flexibility (quantity and type) and economies of scale developed through task specialisation of each of its suppliers (Mabey et al., 2000 p. 177). [5]Outsourcing also allows Gap to focus on its core processes. [6]These include designing clothes, marketing, distribution and sales. [7]Gap does not create value during the manufacturing process. [8]Just as Nike does not consider itself as a manufacturer of sports shoes, Gap is not a manufacturer of leisure clothing.	[1]Gap has recognised that the manufacturing process does not make its product 'unique'. [2]Consequently, it does not own any of the factories that make its goods. [3]Instead Gap's management has made the decision to 'outsource', i.e. sub-contract production to external, independent companies world-wide. [4]This gives Gap a number of advantages. [5]It: • Avoids investment in manufacturing infrastructure • Results in lower manufacturing costs by sourcing from low-cost producers • Enables poor quality products to be rejected • Gives increased flexibility of supply which can be increased or reduced according to demand [6]In human resource management terms outsourcing is considered a 'hard' approach focussing on cost reductions and efficiencies.

(Source: Extract B is from Text 6.1 and Extract C is from Text 6.3 in Resource Book 1)

Compare your answers with those suggested in the Answer section.

Comment

Both of these assignments were very successful but they show how writers can summarise the same case study differently. There are differences in the selection, the reduction and the organisation. Extract B contains more information than Extract C. It uses more business studies concepts and it reduces the case study information to noun groups more than Extract C. Extract C begins with the information that the manufacturing process does not make Gap's products unique. Extract B ends with this information. Extract B uses this information to introduce the idea of *core processes*. Extract B builds on this idea in the next section which compares core processes with periphery processes. Extract C uses a different idea to introduce the next section: the idea of *a hard approach to human resource management*. The two writers organise the information differently to suit their purposes and the analysis they are making.

Successful analyses can summarise the original case study differently and still be successful. However, it is also possible to summarise a case study unsuccessfully. Selecting the wrong information, reducing the information to the wrong word groups and organising the information unclearly can all lead to an unsuccessful analysis. Success depends on the evaluation skills of judgement: on how successfully you select, reduce and organise your summary of the input case study.

6.8 Evidence

Why should you refer to the case study at all in your analysis? The answer is because it is evidence. An analysis which does not contain information from the case study will be difficult to read and will not be persuasive. This was obvious in Session 5. Miriam summarised information about partnership sourcing from the Toyota case study in order to:

- explain partnership sourcing
- demonstrate why she judged partnership sourcing to be a solution for Gap
- persuade her tutor that she understood the issues.

Activity 6.8   ....

Purpose: to notice how evidence from the case study is used in the analysis.

Task: Extracts D and E are from the same analyses you studied in Activity 6.7 (by Stefan and Santosh). Both of these extracts introduce the concept of *corporate culture*.

(a) One extract first gives evidence from the case study about how Gap treats its staff and then introduces the concept of *corporate culture*. The other extract introduces the concept of *corporate culture* first and then gives evidence from the case study to show how Gap treats its staff. Which extract is which?

(b) Which extract gives more details about how Gap treats its staff?

(c) Each extract uses a second key business concept to explain why Gap treats its staff in this way. The key concept is different in each extract. What is the key concept for each?

Extract D – Stefan	**Extract E – Santosh**
Because outsourcing involves the crossing of organisational boundaries, Gap does not have to concern itself too deeply with the human resource management implications for non-Gap employees working in the manufacturing process, which as I have already suggested, is a peripheral process. ... This situation can be contrasted with Gap's own employees who enjoy excellent working conditions and receive an array of benefits above and beyond pay and holiday. For example, they have good career prospects, access to a heath and well being programme and may receive financial assistance for things like moving house, travel and study. The reason for the difference is that Gap's own workers are involved in core processes. They can therefore be labelled as 'core' workers and are viewed as an essential resource of the company. The market for employees who possess 'core' skills is fiercely competitive so Gap must seek to establish a human resources approach geared at attracting, retaining and motivating its employees.	In human resource management terms outsourcing is considered a 'hard' approach focusing on cost reductions and efficiencies. By contrast Gap's style of management of its own staff those involved in its core activities (design, marketing, distribution and retail) is more in line with the 'soft' side of human resource management which 'stresses the importance of empowering staff, of ensuring their commitment, of releasing their creativity and energy' (B200 Study Guide 4, p. 27) as Gap themselves acknowledge 'It takes thousands of passionate, dedicated and talented employees to deliver the merchandise and shopping experience our customers expect and deserve' (Minding the Gap, p. 11). Gap appears to have brought into the message of supporters of 'corporate culture'. Gaining the support and commitment of employees, giving them a 'sense of belonging ... a sense of excitement in the job' (Thompson and McHugh, 2001, p. 142) can directly affect an organisation's performance.

One facet of an HRM approach to staff management is the concept of corporate culture which can loosely be defined as a set of shared values and beliefs aimed at promoting greater levels of enthusiasm and commitment within the organisation. In this regard, Gap's staff management, can be seen as vehicle for achievement and is designed to have a positive psychological impact on human inputs to extract a greater quality of output.

Gap considers it sufficiently important that employees can relate to the company's values and goals that it has introduced a rewards and recognition programme where employees are acknowledged not only for their individual performance, but also for their support of company goals with President's awards being given to outstanding employees (Minding the Gap, p. 11), all backed up by an impressive range of benefits including health care, family support, personal development and career planning and financial assistance.

Its support for those who do volunteer work in the community and donations through Gap Foundation to charitable organisations also help to promote the feeling that Gap is a company with values which employees are proud to be associated with.

(Sources: Extract D is from Text 6.1 and Extract E is from Text 6.3 in Resource Book 1)

Compare your answers with those sugested in the Answer section.

Comment ....

Both Stefan and Santosh frame this part of their analysis with the concept **corporate culture**. This is a very high-level abstract concept. In order to explain what it means and why they think it is important in the analysis, they have to bring evidence from the case study. In other words, they need lower-level details as well as the high-level concept. Both students do this but they organise the information in a different pattern. In Extract D Stefan gives the evidence first and then frames it with the concept. In Extract E Santosh gives the concept first and then explains it with detailed evidence.

Both of these assignments are successful assignments. Both Stefan and Santosh persuaded their tutors to 'buy' their analysis. To do this, they used their judgement to choose evidence from the case study. Then they used the evidence to explain their analysis but they organised their analyses differently. Stefan puts the evidence first because he wants to link the management section to the concept he introduced at the end of the outsourcing section – **core and periphery staff**. Santosh does not use this concept in her section on outsourcing so cannot link the two sections in this way. Instead she uses human resource management (HRM) theory to make the link – outsourcing is a **hard approach to HRM** and *corporate culture is a* **soft approach to HRM**.

6.9 Different perspectives on the case study

Session 4 suggested that problems can be interpreted differently by different people. In fact, case studies can be based on the viewpoints of owners, management, customers, unions, business analysts and others. Here is an example from Text 3.4 in Session 3:

> Workers on average earn about 650,000 pesos ($1,330) per month, said Cipriano a union director. The union said its 2,052 members represent about 94 per cent of the mine's workers. According to Escondida's management, the union represents 70 per cent of the mine's workers.

This includes viewpoints of the union and the management about the number of union members at Escondida. They are all stakeholders and hence have a particular viewpoint of the organisation. Recognising the viewpoints in the case study may be an essential part of the analysis.

Activity 6.9 ....

Purpose: to recognise the range of viewpoints in a case study.

Task: in Session 4, you identified a range of viewpoints in a SWOT analysis of Gap. The sentences below have been taken from the section of the Gap case study 'Gap goes into decline?' Each extract introduces some information in the case study. Each piece of information is the view of a person or an organisation. Find each extract in the case study. How many *different* people or organisations have a view?

Gap goes into decline?

(a) The Guardian (18 November, 2000) reported as follows ...

(b) Initially it was felt that ...

(c) Wendy Liebmann, president of WSL Strategic Retail, a firm of market analysts, said: ...

(d) While Gap was not the only clothing company to have suffered from the downturn in consumer confidence, others seemed relatively unscathed.

(e) For Gap however, ...

(f) By September executives were admitting that ...

(g) ... many stock market analysts criticized the company for ...

(h) Mickey Drexler, the chief executive, assured them that: ...

(i) Shareholders were critical of ...

(j) Analysts, such as Wendy Liebmann, backing Drexler's assessment ...

(k) By Christmas 2001, it had become evident that ...

(l) As the Guardian (23rd November, 2001) reported, ...

(m) This time Gap's senior executives felt ...

(n) ... a Gap spokesperson was quoted as saying ...

(o) To some, Gap's troubles indicated that ...

Compare your answers with those suggested in the Answer section.

Comment ....

This activity showed that a case writer uses various viewpoints to write the case study. For case study purposes, it may be important to see how these voices are incorporated in the case: as a fact, a claim or an accusation. For example, the *Guardian* report is presented almost as a fact while the viewpoints of Gap's management are reported as a claim. Once you recognise their role, you can decide which viewpoints are valuable to your analysis. It will be important to make it clear whose viewpoint you are presenting.

Figure 6.5 illustrates the process of analysing a case study.

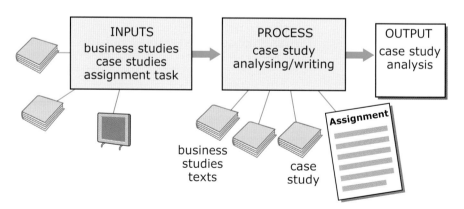

Figure 6.5   Summary of the process of analysing a case study

6.10   Referencing case studies and course books

As you saw in the previous section, the information in a case study can come from various source materials. These can include newspaper reports, company announcements, business analyst reports, shareholders' comments and other people or organisations. Usually, the case study makes it clear where information comes from.

You have to do the same in your analysis. If you are using information from the case study as evidence, or you are using a concept from a business studies course book to explain your analysis, a tutor expects to see where the information comes from.

Activity 6.10 ....

Purpose: to introduce referencing.

Task: in Extract F there are two examples of referencing. One is a reference to the course book. The other is a reference to the case study.

Underline the information which is referred to. Draw a box round the words which tell you where the information comes from.

Extract F

Gap's style of management of its own staff is more in line with the 'soft' side of human resource management which 'stresses the importance of empowering staff, of ensuring their commitment, of releasing their creativity and energy' (B200 Study Guide 4, p. 27). As Gap themselves acknowledge 'It takes thousands of passionate, dedicated and talented employees to deliver the merchandise and shopping experience our customers expect and deserve' (Minding the Gap, p. 11).

Compare your answers with those suggested in the Answer section.

Comment ....

The kind of referencing in this extract is called **quoting**. It presents exactly the same words as were used in the case study or the course book. To show this the words are put in **quotation marks** ('...'). When you quote, you must put the name of the author of the text where you found the quote or, if there is no author's name, the name of the text. The two texts referred to in Extract F do not have author's names. When you reference a quotation, you also have to give the page number of the quotation.

Referencing is an important part of business studies generally and is especially important in essay and report writing. This section gives a brief introduction.

There are three main skills in referencing:

1   deciding what to reference
2   making sure the reference fits into the analysis
3   making it clear that it is a reference.

Deciding what to reference

Deciding what to reference is a part of the total processing of the case study you have practised in this book. Your analysis might refer to anything which you have mapped, framed or identified cause-and-effect or problem and solution for. Exactly what you choose depends on how you understand the purpose of the assignment you are doing.

Making the reference fit into the analysis

Making the reference fit into the analysis will again depend on how you understand the assignment and how you are presenting the analysis. Both Stefan and Santosh make references to the case study and to the course books.

There are two main reasons for referring to the case study.

1   If you include facts and figures in your analysis.

In 1997, Americans bought nearly 350 million pairs of training shoes (Sturges, 2000, p. 11).

2   If you make a judgement about the company's actions.

There are three aspects of their business which Nike must carefully consider (Sturges, 2000, p. 39).

There are three main reasons for referring to the course books.

3   To define or explain a concept.

According to Capon, external environment is the entire context in which a company operates (Capon, 2004, p. 278).

4   To justify framing a case using a concept.

To analyse Nike's impact on developing countries, we will use the concept of 'power' presented by Coates (see Coates, 2000, p. 179).

5   To justify a judgement about the company's actions.

The relationship between Nike and the government is likely to last for a long time because, 'disengaging government and business will be slow and involved' (Min Chen, 2000, p. 203).

Activity 6.11   ....

Purpose: to begin thinking about what to refer to in an analysis.

Task: look again at Extracts B and E. Identify all the places where there is a reference to the case study or the course book. For each one, decide why Stefan or Santosh made a reference at that point in their analysis. Use the list of reasons for referencing above and number each reference.

Compare your answers with those suggested in the Answer section.

Comment   ....

Most of what you write will come from your reading of a case study or the course books. You always have to decide how often you are going to say where the information comes from. In fact, Stefan and Santosh probably do not say where their information has come from enough. However, they said it enough to satisfy their tutors.

Making it clear that it is a reference

Most of the references in these extracts are to quotations. When references are quoted, it is easy to see that the reference comes from another text. However, quoting is not the most common way to refer to another text, as you will see in the next activity.

The next extract comes from a student-analysis of a different case study. As you have not read this case study you may find the analysis difficult to read. However, it is not necessary to understand the analysis to do the activity.

Activity 6.12   ....

Purpose: to notice some different ways of referring to other texts in an analysis.

Task: Extract 6.2 in Resource Book 1 is an extract from an analysis. Underline all the references you can see. How many different ways of referring to another text are there in this analysis?

Compare your answers with those suggested in the Answer section.

Comment   ....

The task of referring to other texts involves a process of evaluation. Before you can refer to the text, you need to decide why you want to refer to it, what you want to refer to, and how you want to refer to it (by summarising or using the exact words).

When referring to another text, you need to acknowledge accurately, giving the details of the source of the information. As you have seen, you must give the last name of the author(s), followed by the year of publication and the page number if applicable. You also need to give the full details in a bibliography at the end of your case study.

6.11 Recommendation and the language of evaluation

In Session 5, you studied some of the language for proposing solutions. Section 5.10 and Activity 5.11 introduced modal verbs, for example:

- It *may be* beneficial
- If Gap *was* interested *it would have to reduce*
- Vendors *could be selected*.

Modal verbs are part of the language of evaluation. They are used to recommend your ideas to other people. In other words, they are a way of persuading people.

This last section on evaluation looks at how evaluation language is used to persuade a reader to accept your analysis. Up to now, you have concentrated on the organisation – or design – of the analysis; but to persuade your reader to accept your analysis, you have to do more than organise it persuasively. You have to **use language persuasively**.

There are many ways in which English can be used persuasively. This section introduces some of them.

As mentioned above, evaluation language is the language of judging, explaining and persuading. This section looks particularly at language for:

- Explaining how you are doing your analysis; for example, *As I have already suggested ...*
- Explaining degrees of possibility: for example, *They may receive financial assistance.*
- Naming something judgementally: for example, *excellent working conditions.*

In Stefan's analysis there are 35 examples of evaluation language. The next three activities look at some of these examples.

Language for explaining how you are doing your analysis

Explaining what you are doing is persuasive for two reasons.

1   You make it clear to the reader how to read your analysis.
2   You show the reader that you are a person, like them. In other words, you have a relationship with them.

There is a good example of explaining how you are doing your analysis at the beginning of Stefan's analysis: *This analysis will compare the two policies starting with an overview of outsourcing.*

This is a simple statement of how the analysis is organised. However, because Stefan tells his reader – who is his tutor – what he is doing, he has begun a relationship with them. This will be useful later in the analysis when he wants to deal with more complicated ideas, for example:

> Gap does not have to concern itself too deeply with the human resource management implications for non-Gap employees working in the manufacturing process which, as I have already suggested, is a peripheral process.

Again, he explains what he is doing by reminding his reader of how he is building this analysis.

Activity 6.13   ....

Purpose: to notice how a writer explains his analysis to their reader.

Task: the following explanation word groups are in Stefan's analysis (Text 6.1). They are from the list of 35 evaluation word groups in his analysis. The numbers show where each of them comes in the list. Find them in the text. Tick the ones you think you would use in an analysis. Put a cross against any that you don't think you would use.

(1)   This analysis will compare

(7)   as I have already suggested,

(9)   can be contrasted with

(14) They can therefore be labelled as

(16) can loosely be defined as

(17) can be seen as

(21) This implies that

(24) It can be regarded as

(32) was elucidated and reasons given to explain why

(33) It was then argued that

(34) using the concept of corporate culture to highlight these differences

(35) it was suggested

There are no suggested answers for this activity.

Comment

Writers have their own ways of explaining what they are doing in a text. You may not want to use some of Stefan's words: for example, *elucidated* or *labelled*. However, some of these words would be useful in most analyses: for example, *suggested* or *can be regarded*.

Language for explaining degrees of possibility

It is not easy to be 100% certain in an analysis. Session 4 on identifying problems, for example, made it clear that analysing problems depends on your viewpoint. So, it is more persuasive if you make it clear that you know this. One way is to use the language of possibility as well as the language of certainty.

In the following extract there are two examples of possibility language.

> Peripheral employees **are likely to be** unskilled, poorly paid and carry out menial, repetitive tasks. This situation **can be contrasted** with Gap's own employees who enjoy excellent working conditions.

There may be several reasons why Stefan wrote *are likely to be*. One possibility is that he does not have definite information about the peripheral employees, whereas he does have about Gap's employees. It is more persuasive not to claim certainty when evidence is not certain.

Can be contrasted is an example of language for explaining how Stefan is doing the analysis. Here, it is more persuasive to say *this situation can be contrasted* than to be more definite and say it *must* or *should be contrasted*. Stefan is trying to persuade his reader to make a contrast, not force them to do it. So he presents it as one possibility among other possibilities.

Activity 6.14

*Spend about
15 minutes on
this activity*

Purpose: to notice how a writer explains degree of possibility.

Task: the following word groups are from Stefan's analysis (Text 6.1). They all explain degrees of possibility. Each one is numbered. Use the numbers to find them in the text. For each one, try a different word with a higher or lower level of uncertainty and decide whether it fits the analysis.

(3)   can lead to

(6)   does not have to concern itself too deeply

(8)   are likely to be

(13) may receive

(22) it must allow

(29) might lead

(30) can help with

(31) can bring down

There are no suggested answers for this activity.

Comment

This session is an introduction to the language of possibility and certainty. This is important language for persuading readers and, therefore, important for professional communication.

Language for naming something judgementally

Every time you name something in an analysis, you are probably making a judgement. For example, underline the judgement words in the following noun groups.

   a difficult year for airlines

   excellent working conditions

   good career prospects

   core workers

   a comparable policy

Sometimes the judgement is in the noun or verb you choose: *crisis* or *difficulty*; *fell* or *dropped*. Sometimes the judgement is in the adjective or adverb that you choose to go with it: *serious* crisis, *small* difficulty; fell *slowly*; dropped *rapidly*. In the noun groups above, the evaluation words are all adjectives.

Every judgement you make in the analysis will influence your reader and persuade them to 'buy' your analysis.

Activity 6.15

Purpose: to notice judgement language in an analysis.

Task: the following word groups are from Stefan's analysis (Text 6.1). They all name things judgementally. Each one is numbered. Use the numbers to find them in the text. For each one, decide whether there other words with the same judgement which could be used?

(10) excellent working conditions

(11) an array of benefits

(12) good career prospects

(15) fiercely competitive

(18) a positive psychological impact

(19) a greater quality of output

(25) automated, impersonal, and in many respects bureaucratic

There are no suggested answers for this activity.

Comment

Sometimes there are several different words which have the same judgement and can be used to name something. However, sometimes it is important to choose judgement words carefully because they affect whether your reader will accept your analysis.

The next activity is based on Santosh's analysis. You read extracts from this in Activities 6.7 and 6.8.

Activity 6.16

Purpose: to practise using evaluation language in an analysis.

Task: the following lists of word groups are from Santosh's analysis (Text 6.3 in Resource Book 1). There are gaps in the text where they have been taken from. Write each word group in the gap in the text where you think it belongs.

Language for explaining how Santosh is doing her analysis

(a) appears to take two different approaches

(b) is considered

(c) is more in line with

(d) appears to have

(e) It is however too simple to say

(f) What is important is that

(g) How effective this Code is however is less obvious

(h) it is difficult to see how

(i) It still appears that

(j) The success of this policy has been witnessed

(k) do appear to exhibit

(l) differences are also evident

Language for explaining degrees of possibility

(m) can directly affect

(n) may consider themselves

(o) they may not even be

Language for naming something judgementally

(p) number of advantages

(q) an impressive range of benefits

(r) a company with values which employees are proud to be associated with

(s) a comparable 'conduct' policy

(t) a structural approach to the employment process

(u) good salaries and an extensive range of benefits

(v) poor working conditions, low salaries and a vulnerability

Compare your answers with those suggested in the Answer section.

Comment ....

The language of evaluation runs through an analysis. As you have just seen with Stefan's and Santosh's texts, the same assignment title can lead to different outputs. This includes using different evaluation language. However, although there are differences in the evaluation language, they both depend on using evaluation language skilfully.

6.12 Vocabulary activity

See the course website for how to do a vocabulary-building activity for this session.

6.13 Review

This session focused on the sixth skill in case study analysis: evaluation. It also reviewed the five skills practised in Sessions 1 to 5. In particular, you have developed your skills in:

- writing a compare-and-contrast case analysis to communicate with your audience according to assignment instructions and concepts

- summarising as a form of evaluation

- recognising different points of view in a case study

- using data from the case study as evidence in the analysis

- referring to case studies and business studies texts in an analysis

- using the language of evaluation to judge, explain and persuade.

6.14 Conclusion

We hope that, now you have completed this book, you will be more confident and better equipped to analyse business cases. Sessions 1 to 4 concentrated on input texts and the analysis process. Sessions 5 and 6 were more concerned with the output texts – the case analyses which you present to your course tutor.

During the course, we have often referred to what your tutor expects from you when you analyse a business case. Sometimes you might have wondered why it is necessary to think about what your tutor expects. Surely it is your ideas which are important, not your tutor's expectations? This is true. There is not one single correct way to do an analysis and, as you have seen, different students can produce different analyses from the same assignment title.

However, as you have also seen, there are similarities between high-scoring analyses for two reasons.

1   Analysis is a process based on a range of shared business concepts and business texts. It is a way of business thinking. Business thinkers do not all reach the same conclusions but they

do share many of the same ways of thinking. The purpose of business case analysis is to develop those ways of thinking.

2   The skills of business analysis are professional communication skills. Successful communication is very dependent on your understanding of your audience and your context. Your reader is your tutor. The context is business studies and the world of business. The more understanding you have of your tutor's expectations and the context, the more successful your communication will be. This book has concentrated on some of those expectations and that context.

However, this book could not deal with all the possibilities. Each business course, business tutor and business case assignment has its own expectations and context. As a professional communicator, your success depends on understanding these. There is no single formula.

The next two books in this course build on this one. The output texts you produce when you analyse a business case are usually reports or essays. As you will see, the analysis you have practised in this book is the basis of successful reports and essays.

6.15 Critical reflection

The following statements are critical of the approach taken in this book. What do you think of them? Write some responses to them in your Learning Journal.

1   The most important skill in analysing a business case is creative thinking. You cannot learn creative thinking.

2   Analysing a business case is something you do to develop your own thinking. If you worry about your tutor's expectations too much, you will not develop yourself.

3   There are very many different kinds of business cases and very many different business concepts. You cannot learn how to do business case analysis in a general way. You have to learn it again for each new business case you analyse.

4   It is not very useful to read other students' business case analyses because every student is different.

5   Analysing business cases is not a professional communication skill.

6   Language is not an important part of business case analysis.

6.16 Answer section

Activity 6.2

1   Gap has a supply chain spread over more than 50 countries. There are over 3000 factories to oversee.
2   Gap has found it difficult to manage the vendors successfully.
3   The writer proposes that Gap should integrate the vendor into the Gap system.

Activity 6.3

1 (d); 2 (c); 3 (a); 4 (b).

Activity 6.4

1   Compare and contrast Gap's staff management with its outsourcing policy.
2(a) Staff management policy: The way a company treats its staff.
2(b) Outsourcing policy: The way a company contracts out some of its activity to other companies.

Activity 6.5

1   *To optimise performance*; that is, to produce the best quality outputs with the least costly inputs and processes.
2   *Externalisation of the production process.*
3   *Cheaper sources of the routine labour required in the manufacturing process.*
4   *Competitive advantage, cost reduction, output flexibility, economies of scale through task specialisation.* (You were asked to name only one.)
5   Design clothes, marketing, distribution and sales.
6   *Outsourcing allows Gap to focus on its core processes.* This implies that manufacturing is a peripheral process – that is, not core.
7   Core employees – excellent conditions, benefits and pay; good career prospects, access to health and wellbeing programme, financial assistance for moving house.

     Peripheral employees – unskilled, poorly paid, menial, repetitive tasks.

     (You were asked to name only one for each.)

8   A fiercely competitive market
9   *Gap must seek to establish a human resources approach geared at attracting, retaining and motivating its employees.*
10   Corporate culture is *designed to have a positive psychological impact on human inputs and to extract a greater quantity of output.*

11   Gap must allow suppliers to determine their own human resource strategy; the fact that there are few job opportunities means suppliers do not have to win the hearts and minds of their employees.

12   *Market forces (market demand or job (in)security).*

13   Three

Activity 6.6

The corrected notes should say:

[P6]   Subheading frames section with second main concept, *staff management* and introduces new key concept *core versus periphery*.

[P7]   Explains *contrast* (instead of Explains similarity).

[P8]   Moves back to *outsourcing* concept. Uses cause–effect to explain.

[P9]   Subheading introduces two new concepts.

[P12] Repeats explanation of contrast analysis framed by concept of *corporate culture*.

Activity 6.7

1 Selection

(a)   [Extract C] Results in lower manufacturing costs by sourcing from low-cost producers = [Extract B] cost reduction, (labour and materials)

[Extract C] Gives increased flexibility of supply which can be increased or reduced according to demand = [Extract B] output flexibility (quantity and type).

(b)   No

(c)   Yes: *economies of scale developed through task specialisation of each of its suppliers (Mabey et al., 2000, p. 177).*

(d)   Yes: in the last four sentences.

2 Reduction

(a)   Extract C: sub-contract production to external, independent companies world-wide.

Extract B: the externalisation of its production processes

(b)   competitive advantage

(c)   cost reduction, (labour and materials), output flexibility (quantity and type)

(d)   economies of scale developed through task specialisation of each of its suppliers

(e)   effective management of the supply chain

Activity 6.8

(a)   Extract D gives evidence first.

(b)   Extract E gives more details.

Extract E: a rewards and recognition programme; President's awards for outstanding employees; range of benefits including health care, family support, personal development and career planning and financial assistance; support for volunteer work in the community; donations to charitable organisations.

Extract D: excellent working conditions; an array of benefits above and beyond pay and holiday; good career prospects; access to a health and wellbeing programme; financial assistance for moving house, travel and study.

(c)   Extract D: *core workers*; Extract E: *'soft' side of human resource management*

Activity 6.9

Five different people or organisations have viewpoints as follows.

1   **The Guardian**: (a) The Guardian (18th November, 2000) reported as follows; (l) As the Guardian (23rd November, 2001) reported ...

2   **The company executives**: (f) By September executives were admitting that; (h) Mickey Drexler, the chief executive, assured them that; (m) This time Gap's senior executives felt; (n) a Gap spokesperson was quoted as saying.

3   **Shareholders:** (i) Shareholders were critical of.

4   **The stock market analysts**: (g) many stock market analysts criticized the company for; (c) Wendy Liebmann, president of WSL Strategic Retail, a firm of market analysts, said; (j) Analysts, such as Wendy Liebmann, backing Drexler's assessment; (o) To some, Gap's troubles indicated that.

5   **The case study writer** (although sometimes it is not clear whether they are expressing other people's viewpoints): (b) Initially it was felt that; (d) While Gap was not the only clothing company to have suffered from the downturn in consumer confidence, others seemed relatively unscathed; (e) For Gap however; (k) By Christmas 2001, it had become evident that.

Activity 6.10

Gap's style of management of its own staff, is more in line with the 'soft' side of human resource management which "stresses the importance of empowering staff, of ensuring their commitment, of releasing their creativity and energy" (B200 Study Guide 4, p. 27). As Gap themselves acknowledge 'It takes thousands of passionate, dedicated and talented employees to deliver the merchandise and shopping experience our customers expect and deserve' (Minding the Gap, p. 11).

Activity 6.11

Extract B

(3, maybe 4)

Effective management of the supply chain can lead to competitive advantage through cost reduction, (labour and materials), output flexibility (quantity and type) and economies of scale developed through task specialisation of each of its suppliers (Mabey et al., 2000, p. 177).

Extract E

(1) Gap's style of management of its own staff, is more in line with the 'soft' side of human resource management which 'stresses the importance of empowering staff, of ensuring their commitment, of releasing their creativity and energy' (B200 Study Guide 4, p. 27).

(3) As Gap themselves acknowledge 'It takes thousands of passionate, dedicated and talented employees to deliver the merchandise and shopping experience our customers expect and deserve' (Minding the Gap, p. 11).

(4 and 5) Gap appears to have bought into the message of supporters of 'corporate culture'. Gaining the support and commitment of employees, giving them a "sense of belonging ... a sense of excitement in the job" (Thompson and McHugh, *Organisations*, p. 142) can directly affect an organisation's performance.

(1) Gap considers it sufficiently important that employees can relate to the company's values and goals that it has introduced a rewards and recognition programme where employees are acknowledged not only for their individual performance, but also for their support of company goals with President's awards being given to outstanding employees (Minding the Gap, p. 11).

Activity 6.12

The exact number depends on how you group them. It is possible to find 11 types as follows.

1   as a result of the Asda takeover <u>(Costello, 1995, p.86)</u>
      Expansion allows for broader activities to be carried out within the organisation <u>(Costello, 1995, p.85–86).</u>

2   <u>'It took Wal-Mart ....a gold mine, in Britain' (Levine, 2004, p.80)</u>
      <u>This is evidenced by</u> 'expanding sales from $16.8 billion in 1999 to $21.7billion [in 2003]' <u>(Levine, 2004, p.80)</u>
      culminating in Wal-Mart becoming the 'largest company and the biggest employer in the world' <u>(p.2).</u>

3   sales and retail space growth <u>as explained in the case study (Asda-Wal-Mart case study, p.6),</u>

4   Although initial investment was costly (£6.7billion <u>according to Wal-Mart's Annual Report 2000)</u>

5   <u>Sloman and Sutcliffe, however, argue that</u> co-ordination .... become longer and more complex" <u>(1998, p.204).</u>

6   <u>They also suggest that</u> language ... into a foreign market <u>(p.203)</u>

7   problems experienced in Germany <u>(Asda-Wal-Mart case study, p.6).</u>

8   <u>Sloman and Sutcliffe (1998, p.204) do point to</u> the perceived imposition of foreign strategies

9   <u>Whysall highlights</u> the points of contrast ... 'a wide range of general merchandise' (Whysall, 2001, p.731)

10   <u>However, he also explains that</u> .... 'a wide selection of discounted merchandise' (2001, p.733).

11   <u>The case study reflects</u> this latter point, <u>stating that,</u> 'there was always going to be a good fit between Asda and Wal-Mart' <u>(Asda-Wal-Mart case study, p.4)</u>

Activity 6.16

(1) appears to take two different approaches

(5) is considered

(7) is more in line with

(8) appears to have

(13) It is however too simple to say

(15) What is important is that

(16) How effective this Code is however is less obvious

(17) it is difficult to see how

(21) It still appears that

(23) The success of this policy has been witnessed

(24) do appear to exhibit

(25) differences are also evident.

(9) can directly affect

(18) may consider themselves

(20) they may not even be

(4) number of advantages

(11) an impressive range of benefits

(12) a company with values which employees are proud to be associated with

(22) a comparable 'conduct' policy

(25) a structural approach to the employment process

(27) good salaries and an extensive range of benefits

(28) poor working conditions, low salaries and a vulnerability

References

Cherrington, D. J. (1995) *The Management of Human Resources*, Englewood Cliffs, NJ, Prentice-Hall.

Easton, G. (1992) *Learning from Case Studies*, New York, Prentice-Hall.

Finlay, P. N. (2000) *Strategic Management: An Introduction to Business and Corporate Strategy*, Harlow, Financial Times/Prentice Hall.

Acknowledgements

Grateful acknowledgement is made to the following sources:

Illustrations/photographs

Page 76: Copyright © Mike Baldwin/Cornered; page 108: Copyright © Rex Features; page 125: © Najlah Feanny/Corbis; page 169: © Getty Images/Photodisc; page 171: www.mobilerainbow.co.uk.

Index

Entries in **bold type** are defined in the course Glossary.